Writing

An Art- and Literature-Based Approach

Sharon Sorenson

AMSCO SCHOOL PUBLICATIONS, INC.
315 Hudson Street/New York, N.Y. 10013

As an English teacher and department chair in Indiana, Sharon Sorenson has taught the art of writing to over 1,000 students. She has also taught at the University of Evansville and written twelve books for students and teachers. She is presently a full-time writer, lecturer, and in-service instructor for high school teachers.

Cover: Edward Hopper, *The Lighthouse at Two Lights*. The Metropolitan Museum of Art, Hugo Kastor Fund, 1962. (62.95)
Photograph © 1990 The Metropolitan Museum of Art

When ordering this book, please specify:
either R 654 W or WRITING: AN ART- AND LITERATURE-BASED APPROACH

ISBN 1-56765-048-1
NYC Item 56765-047-1

To the Teacher

A POET ONCE SAID, "We read with our ears." It is clear we can hear the words we read if they have the music that includes other senses besides sight. Good writing and enjoyable reading involve all of our senses. Who can forget the first page of Charles Dickens' epic tale of the French revolution *A Tale of Two Cities*, once read? The beauty and sound of his words ring in our ears long after the pages have slipped from our fingers.

The philosophy that calls for the integration of the language arts came about because educators discovered that people learn language rules best in context, not as isolated bits of information. For example, vocabulary study is more easily understood when we experience words in well-written sentences and well-constructed paragraphs. Grammar, usage, and the mechanics of writing are much easier to grasp when we see how fine writers apply these skills. We can then model our own writing after those whose work we admire.

Integration is supported when we consider language arts as part of the all-encompassing term "fine arts." The language arts enable writers to convey powerful messages: this resulting fine art of literature becomes a model of quality by which we can learn. In this larger picture, the fine arts of painting, sculpting, and photography, for example, contain many of the same elements as does literature: conflict, plot, setting, character, mood, tone, insight, action, symbolism, and so on.

By design, this book begins each chapter with fine-arts visual avenues that lead directly into the fine art of literature. In turn, the literature functions as a model that provides students access to the language arts. Supported by step-by-step guidance through the writing process; tips for punctuation, spelling, and capitalization; connections to interdisciplinary and workplace skills; and hints for computer and Internet use, each chapter integrates the fine arts and language arts for student success. The skills chart on pages 226–227 testifies to the thorough instructional development present in each strand.

Contents

LITERARY ACKNOWLEDGMENTS

VISUAL ART ACKNOWLEDGMENTS

ELIZABETH CATLETT, *Cartas*. Hampton University Museum, Hampton, Virginia. © 1997 Elizabeth Catlett/Licensed by VAGA, New York.

JULES GUERIN, *Flatiron Building*. © 1996, The Art Institute of Chicago, gift of Thomas J. and Mary Eyerman Foundation.

JEAN ANTOINE WATTEAU, *The Old Savoyard*. © 1996, The Art Institute of Chicago; Helen Regenstein Collection.

ANSEL ADAMS, *Flock in Owens Valley*. National Archives and Records Administration, Still Picture Branch.

VINCENT VAN GOGH, *Shoes*. The Metropolitan Museum of Art, Annenberg Foundation Gift.

TORII KIYOMASU I, *Sparrow Hawk*. © 1996, The Art Institute of Chicago, Clarence Buckingham Collection.

ANDRÉ KERTÉSZ, *Mondrian's Glasses and Pipe*. © Estate of André Kertész.

JOHN BIGGERS, *Drummers of Ede*. Courtesy of the artist.

GEORGIA O'KEEFFE, *Cow's Skull with Calico Roses*. © 1996, The Art Institute of Chicago.

ANSEL ADAMS, *Taos Pueblo, New Mexico*. National Archives and Records Administration, Still Picture Branch.

FREDERIC REMINGTON, *The Bronco Buster*. © 1996, The Art Institute of Chicago, gift of Burr L. Robbins.

KATSUSHIKA HOKUSAI, *The Great Wave Off Kanagawa*. © 1996, The Art Institute of Chicago, Clarence Buckingham Collection.

ELIZABETH CATLETT, *Shoe Shine Boy*. Hampton University Museum, Hampton, Virginia. © 1997 Elizabeth Catlett/Licensed by VAGA, New York.

CHARLES SHEELER, *Drive Wheels*. © 1993 The Detroit Institute of Arts, Founders Society Purchase, John S. Newberry Fund and J. Lawrence Buell, Jr. Fund.

HUGHIE LEE-SMITH, *The Piper*. Photograph © 1990 The Detroit Institute of Arts, Gift of Mr. and Mrs. Stanley J. Winkelman. © 1996 Hughie Lee-Smith/ Licensed by VAGA, New York.

GUSTAVE CAILLEBOTTE, *Paris Street: Rainy Day*. Charles H. and Mary F.S. Worcester Collection, © 1996 The Art Institute of Chicago. All rights reserved.

RICHARD ESTES, *Cafe Express*. Gift of Mary and Leigh Block, 1988. © 1996, The Art Institute of Chicago. All rights reserved. 1996 © Richard Estes, courtesy, Marlborough Gallery, New York.

NI TSAN, *Woods and Valleys of Yu-shan*. The Metropolitan Museum of Art, Gift of the Dillon Fund, 1973. All rights reserved, The Metropolitan Museum of Art.

PAUL LANTZ, *Snow in Santa Fe*. Gift of the Public Employee Retirement Agency, 1972. Museum of Fine Arts, Museum of New Mexico, Santa Fe.

ELIZABETH CATLETT, *Red Leaves*. Hampton University Museum, Hampton, Virginia. © 1997 Elizabeth Catlett/Licensed by VAGA, New York.

JOHN BIGGERS, *Ma Biggers Quilting*. Courtesy of the artist.

Visual Art Acknowledgments

chapter 1

Finding

Something to Write About

PREWRITING

Visuals

1. "Cartas" by Elizabeth Catlett
2. "Perspective Rendering of the Flatiron Building, New York" by Jules Guerin
3. "The Old Savoyard" by Jean-Antoine Watteau
4. "Flock in Owens Valley, 1941" by Ansel Adams
5. "Shoes" by Vincent van Gogh

"An idea can turn to dust or magic, depending on the talent that rubs against it."
William Bernbach,
advertising executive
New York Times

Your Viewer's Response

Writing ideas are everywhere. You can find them along the street where you live. You can find them in your house or apartment building or at the mall. Like those places, these pictures are filled with ideas.

Choose one picture that you like. Or choose one of your own from a photo album, book, or magazine. What does the picture make you think about? In your learning log, list five ideas that the picture suggests to you.

As a class, put together a list of writing ideas for each picture.

Cartas by Elizabeth Catlett

Perspective Rendering of the Flatiron Building, New York by Jules Guerin

The Old Savoyard by Antoine Watteau

Shoes by Vincent van Gogh

Flock in Owens Valley, 1941 by Ansel Adams

Reading the Literature

The selection you are about to read shows how one writer kept his eyes open for **details.** One lucky detail gave him an idea for a television news story. It tugged at the hearts of a nation of viewers.

About the Author

Charles Kuralt traveled the back roads of the United States, looking for stories for the nightly television news. One afternoon he saw a banner that said "Welcome Home, Roger!" That lucky detail gave him an idea for a story.

Vocabulary

epigram (EP uh gram) n. a clever saying

beekeeper (BEE keep er) n. someone who raises honeybees

venerable (VEN er uh buhl) adj. worthy of respect because of age

resonated (REZ uh nayt id) v. made sounds like echoes

switchboard (SWICH bohrd) n. where phone calls are controlled

compelled (kuhm PELD) adj. forced to do something

A LIFE ON THE ROAD
by Charles Kuralt

We have found, in the words of the golfer's epigram, that it's better to be lucky than good.

Once, looking for stories on the back roads of Ohio, we were suffering a week-long dry spell. A colorful beekeeper we'd been told about was away from home when we called on him, visiting a niece in Colorado or someplace. A promising old-time candy store had been sold and turned into a pizza joint. A venerable amusement park where we thought we might find a story had shut down for the season. We began to get a little discouraged.

We passed a farmhouse with a homemade banner stretched between two oak trees in the front yard. The banner said in huge letters: "WELCOME HOME, ROGER!" We drove on for a mile or two. Somebody said, "Wonder who Roger is?"

We turned around, went back there and knocked on the door.

Roger was a soldier on his way home from the Vietnam War. His family knew he was coming, but wasn't sure what day he was going to arrive. Roger's mother was in the kitchen baking his favorite chocolate cake. Really—she was. His wife was there with a baby son Roger hadn't seen. We asked if they'd mind if we brought the camera into the house. Roger's mother said it would be all right if we'd give her a minute to fix her hair. I am sure we weren't there more than an hour, talking to those people who were all excited about Roger coming home. We never did see Roger, of course.

At my desk in the bus as we rolled on that afternoon, I wrote a simple story letting Roger represent all the GIs coming home to their families from Vietnam. We found an airport and shipped the film to New York, and Walter Cronkite put the story on the *Evening News* the next night.

Rarely has any of our stories caused such a reaction from viewers. It was just an account of waiting for Roger, that's all, but it resonated in the country. The CBS switchboard lighted up that night with dozens of calls from people moved by it in some way, and hundreds of letters came in, some of them asking that the story be repeated. There was so much interest nationwide that Cronkite felt compelled to report on the air a few nights later, "Oh, and by the way—Roger got home!"

That hour with Roger's family made it a good trip to Ohio, after all. I had done a fair amount of careful planning in preparation for the week's work, but careful planning got us nowhere. Then along came a banner stretched across a farmhouse yard.

Back at the office, people asked, "How do you *find* these stories?"

"Well," I said, "you do have to work at it."

All you really have to do is look out the window.

Your Reader's Response

Think about Charles Kuralt's experience finding something to write about. As he says, "All you really have to do is look out the window."

What writing ideas could you find if you looked out the window, perhaps at home, at school, in the car or bus? Close your eyes and imagine what you would see. In your learning log, list at least five ideas.

Springboards for Writing

To find more topics, choose one or both of the following activities.

Individual Activity. Kuralt noticed the "Welcome Home, Roger!" banner as he and the other crew members were driving along. Being watchful is a big part of finding topics to write about.

Set a timer for ten minutes. Freewrite as fast as you can about whatever you see. "Freewrite" means two things. First, don't worry about spelling, grammar, or complete sentences. It's even okay to write lists. Second, don't stop writing, even if you must write something such as, "I'm running out of things to write about."

As you freewrite, try to look for details, like a scrap of paper on the floor, a poster, or someone walking by. You may even choose to study another picture at the beginning of this chapter. Look for *your* "lucky" details.

At the end of the ten-minute period, reread what you have written. Underline topics that, like Kuralt's banner or Ansel Adams' flock of sheep, might suggest a writing idea.

Group Activity. Charles Kuralt looked out the window to see the everyday words "welcome home." They gave him an idea to write about. With two or three classmates, think about the everyday words that follow. What ideas do they give you to write about? Think of at least three writing topics for each word.

The first one is done for you.

EXAMPLE: Bus

WRITING IDEAS: cheap travel
why use public transportation?
school-bus ride—time to meet friends

working in a restaurant (bussing)
bus stop as meeting place
waiting for bus in bad weather
characters spotted on bus

basketball	plate	stairs
winter	coast	mouse
vegetables	television	neighbor

Now Decide

From your Viewer's Response, Reader's Response, or the activities above, pick one topic that you would most like to write about. In your learning log, write two sentences about it. Model your sentences after Kuralt's:

> The banner said in huge letters: "Welcome Home, Roger!" . . . Somebody said, "Wonder who Roger is?"

Begin your sentences with, "I noticed . . . This detail made me wonder about . . ."

Studying the Model

Specific Details. If someone besides Kuralt had told the story about Roger, you might have read something like this:

> Kuralt saw a banner and went in to find out about it. Then he wrote a story about a young man coming home from the war.

How dull!

Kuralt, however, uses **specific details** to paint a clear picture. For instance, you know the banner was home-made. You know it was stretched between two trees, and you know what it said. Then you learn about a soldier coming home. You know his name. You know his favorite cake. You meet his wife and son. You know his mother fixed her hair before the cameras were brought in. And you know what happened later. All because Kuralt uses those specific details.

In your learning log, make a list of other specific details Kuralt shares about Roger and his family. About what percent of Kuralt's story do you think is made up of specific details?

If you have access to electronic mail (e-mail) or networked computers, work with a partner at separate terminals. With your partner, or at the direction of your teacher, choose one of the words above. Work three minutes each to come up with writing ideas. Then send your ideas to each other. See who came up with more. Then use these ideas to help you think of even more ideas. Which is the best topic for you?

HINT

Mapping Your Writing: Brainstorm with a Cluster Map

To plan his story, Kuralt might have used a cluster map similar to the one below. Try using one of your own. In the center of your cluster map, write your topic. Then see how many specific details you can map.

CLUSTER MAP FOR CHARLES KURALT

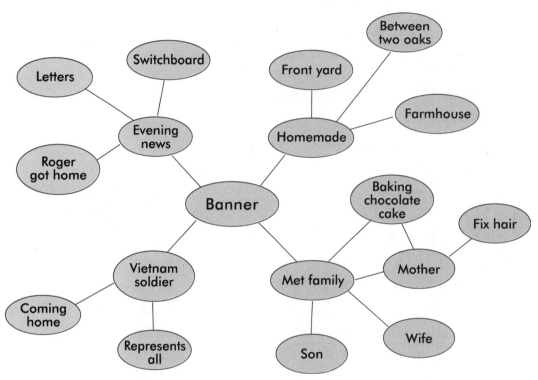

WRITING

Your Assignment

Choose an everyday sight, like the "Welcome Home, Roger!" banner in Kuralt's story or the old pair of shoes in the Van Gogh painting. Write about what you saw. The following activities will help you.

Thinking About the Model

The **specific details** that Kuralt uses paint pictures for you. He writes that, "We passed a farmhouse." Notice, it wasn't just *any* house, but a *farm*house. He writes about a "homemade banner stretched between two oak trees in the

Writing: An Art- and Literature-Based Approach

front yard." This is not a computer-printed banner, but a *homemade* one. It doesn't hang; it's *stretched*. And the trees are *oak* trees. They are not just in the yard, but in the *front* yard.

The specific details help Kuralt explain his general idea. Your cluster map will help you write the same kinds of specific details.

Writing Process Tip: Topic Sentence

A **topic sentence** is a general statement of what you are writing about. It names the **topic** and gives a **clue** as to what the writer will say about that topic.

Kuralt says in his first sentence:

It's better to be lucky than good.

This is Kuralt's topic sentence. His topic? "To be lucky. " The clue? "Better." Everything else Kuralt writes explains *how* it is better to be lucky than good.

Likewise, the topic sentence of the story Cronkite gave on the *Evening News* might have been the following:

Roger represents all Vietnam soldiers returning home. (Subject: *Roger*; clue: *represents*)

Everything in the news story explained *how* Roger represents all Vietnam soldiers returning home.

Write your topic sentence now.

Now Write

Using your topic sentence and cluster map, write the first draft of your paper. Use as many details as you can. Make sure the details explain your topic sentence.

When you finish your first draft, return to the lesson. You will use Kuralt's writing as a model for revising.

REVISING

Checking Model's Map: Specific Details

Specific details explain general ideas. Charles Kuralt begins with the general idea that it is better to be lucky than good. By showing **specific details,** he explains how the lucky experience of driving by a "Welcome Home, Roger!" banner led to a highly successful news story.

Specific words also paint pictures. They help you see color, shape, and size. They also help you hear sounds and feel texture. Look at these specific, picture-making words.

Exact color: pink, teal, scarlet, neon green
Exact shape: rectangular, spiral, crescent
Exact size: speck, mile, block, football field
Exact sound: whisper, growl, whistle, thump
Exact texture: bristles, sandpaper, denim, powder

In your learning log, copy Kuralt's basic cluster map from page 8. Add details from Kuralt's story to show how he paints a picture of his idea.

The following exercises will help you identify and use picture-making details.

Exercise A—Identifying Specific Details

Directions. Look at each pair of sentences. In each pair, one sentence is more specific than the other. In your learning log, number from 1 to 10. Beside each number, write the letter of the more specific sentence.

EXAMPLE:
(*a*) The banner was hanging between two trees.
(*b*) The banner was stretched between two trees.

ANSWER: *b*
("Stretched" gives a clearer picture than "hanging.")

1. (*a*) The evening news told of a soldier returning home from the Vietnam War.
   (*b*) The evening news showed the Vietnam soldier's family welcoming him home.
2. (*a*) Mom baked his favorite chocolate cake and fixed her hair.
   (*b*) Mom baked a cake and fixed herself up to look really pretty.
3. (*a*) The switchboard received numerous calls about the news item.
   (*b*) The switchboard lit up with callers asking about Roger's return.

4. *(a)* Kuralt's news team looked for ideas wherever they were.

   (b) Kuralt's news team eyed every person and place on the road as a possible story.

5. *(a)* Finding topics is often a matter of luck.

   (b) News story ideas are often a matter of luck.

6. *(a)* Since the owners had sold the old-time candy store, Kuralt's story idea was gone.

   (b) Kuralt's story idea about a candy store fell through.

7. *(a)* The time with Roger's family gave Kuralt a good story.

   (b) The hour with Roger's family gave Kuralt a good story.

8. *(a)* A trip along Ohio's back roads failed to give Kuralt's team a good story.

   (b) Careful planning failed to give Kuralt's team a good story.

9. *(a)* The camera crew shipped the film to New York.

   (b) The camera crew air lifted the film to Walter Cronkite.

10. *(a)* Cronkite reported that the Vietnam soldier had come home.

    (b) Cronkite reported, "Roger got home."

Exercise B—Adding Specific Details

Directions. The following sentences need added details. In your learning log, number from 1 to 10. Beside each number, write a detail word to fill in the blank in each sentence. More than one answer can be right.

EXAMPLE: The banner stretched between two _____ trees.
DETAIL: oak

1. How do you think Roger liked the _____ banner in the front yard?

2. Proud neighbors probably watched Roger's _____ homecoming.

3. As she waited, Roger's mom planned a _____ meal.

4. His brother arrived in a new _____ car.

5. _____ classmates were also part of the welcoming committee.

Specific details include proper nouns. Remember to capitalize them. Kuralt uses these proper nouns: Ohio, Colorado, Roger, Vietnam War, New York, Walter Cronkite, *Evening News*, and CBS.

On the other hand, do not capitalize common nouns. The common noun for Ohio is *state*. Can you give the common noun for the other proper nouns Kuralt uses?

6. Roger's _____ son was just ready to take his first steps.

7. Together again, the _____ family will have to get to know each other.

8. Watchful, the neighbors shared the _____ excitement.

9. The news team never mentioned Roger's last name, so he came to represent _____ soldiers.

10. _____ sunshine shone on Roger's arrival.

Exercise C—Making Details Specific

Directions. The following sentences include vague words that can be made more specific. In your learning log, number from 1 to 10. Beside each number, write a more specific word for the vague *italicized* one. More than one answer can be right.

EXAMPLE: The family *hung* a welcome banner across the front yard.

MORE SPECIFIC: stretched

1. Roger *walked* into his wife's open arms.
2. Not wanting to butt in, neighbors *looked* from their windows.
3. Jerry's new *car* was in the driveway.
4. Jerry's new car *was* in the driveway.
5. Mother prepared a *meal* for the whole family.
6. The family *talked* late into the night.
7. The family *dog* came out to greet Roger.
8. The family dog *came* out to greet Roger.
9. *Someone* had the video camera going.
10. The front yard soon filled with *people.*

Exercise D—Writing Specific Details

Directions. In your learning log, number from 1 to 10. See the pictures on pages 2–3 to write sentences with specific details.

1. Describe the woman's eyes in "Cartas."
2. Describe her hands or their position.
3. Tell about the Flatiron Building's location.

COMPUTER

Use an on-line thesaurus to find more specific words for the italicized ones.

HINT

4. Tell how it looks.

5. Describe one piece of the Old Savoyard's clothing.

6. Tell about what he carries.

7. Describe the landscape in which the flock in Owens Valley grazes.

8. Tell about the time of day Ansel Adams pictures the sheep.

9. Tell where the Dutch shoes are sitting.

10. Tell about the shoelaces.

Peer-editor Activity. Ask a peer to read your draft with you to check for specific details. Together, find the specific details in your paper. Highlight them.

Checking the Links: Linking Words and Word Groups

In writing, sentences do not stand alone. They must be linked to one another. Thus, a writer links her ideas so that you can follow her meaning. One way to link meaning is to use linking words and word groups. For instance, Kuralt uses them in these sentences:

Once, looking for stories on the back roads of Ohio, we were suffering a week-long dry spell.

His family knew he was coming, *but* wasn't sure what day he was going to arrive.

We never did see Roger, *of course*.

Other examples of linking words and word groups include the following:

however	as a result	moreover
nevertheless	therefore	besides
on the contrary	thus	that is
consequently	in summary	in addition
then	next	instead

The following exercises will help you understand and use linking words and word groups.

Exercise E—Finding Linking Words

Directions. In your learning log, number from 1 to 5. Find the transitional word or phrase in each of the sentences below. Write it beside the number of the sentence.

EXAMPLE: Roger's classmates were scattered across the country; nevertheless, many sent homecoming greetings to him.

LINK: nevertheless

1. Jerry wanted to buy a new car; however, he worried about making his payments.
2. Jerry hoped for a new car. Instead, he chose a used car.
3. A new car cost more, had more costly insurance and more costly licensing fees. Besides, a used car would have the bugs worked out.
4. In addition, Jerry hoped he could save more money for school.
5. The used car seemed to be the best solution. Consequently, he has money left over from his paycheck each week.

Exercise F—Adding Linking Words

Directions. These sentences need links. In your learning log, number from 1 to 10. For each pair of sentences, choose a linking word or phrase from the list on page 13. Choose links that make the sentences more meaningful.

1. Roger knew there would be danger in the military. _____, he chose to enlist anyway.
2. Mother first baked the cake and let it cool. _____, she iced it.
3. The baby was hungry and tired from the family excitement. _____, he began squirming and crying.
4. Travel into the small town was slow and unreliable; _____, Roger finally arrived.
5. Neighbors were worried about crowds and noise. _____, it turned out to be a quiet homecoming.
6. Most neighbors stopped by later just to say hello. _____, some stayed to visit.

7. Welcome greetings came in cards and flowers. _____, one cousin even sent baseball tickets.

8. Roger thought he was coming home quietly, without fanfare. _____, his family wanted a celebration.

9. Roger had one ambition. _____, he wanted to hold the son he'd never seen.

10. Fortunately, the weather was perfect. _____, the family dinner turned into an outdoor picnic.

Review your draft. Have you used good links? Revise as needed.

Exercise G—Finding Specific Details in Your Writing

Directions. Before you wrote your first draft, you made a cluster map of details you might use. Compare it with your draft. Did you use all of the details? Can you add others? Does every sentence include specific details? Make revisions as needed.

Peer-editor Activity. Ask a peer to read your paper and suggest at least two more places where you can add specific details. Be sure to use links to connect the ideas.

PROOFREADING

Right Reading: Complete Sentences

When you talk with people, you no doubt use incomplete sentences. When you write, though, you should use complete sentences. A complete sentence has a subject and verb, and it gives a complete thought.

EXAMPLES:

Complete:	Why did Roger come home?
Incomplete:	Because the war was over. (Okay for conversation.)
Complete:	Roger came home because the war was over. (Correct for writing.)
Incomplete:	After Roger came home.
Complete:	After Roger came home, he began job hunting.

COMPUTER

Some software applications will let you check your writing for links. Some word processing programs may also include "style checkers." Better programs even have word bins with lists of linking words and phrases that you can click on and drag into your own writing.

HINT

Incomplete sentences, sometimes called "sentence fragments," should not appear in your paper. To practice finding incomplete sentences, try these exercises.

Exercise H—Identifying Complete and Incomplete Sentences

Directions. In your learning log, number from 1 to 10. Study the following groups of words. Five of them are sentences; five are fragments. Place an X next to the numbers of the fragments. Write "okay" next to the numbers of complete sentences.

1. Mom wept.
2. From the first of the war until now.
3. As if they were part of the family, neighbors joined the welcome.
4. Knowing that Roger was coming home but not knowing exactly when, the family planned ahead.
5. Knowing that travel into and out of their small town was neither easy nor reliable.
6. Because Roger had been gone for almost two years.
7. To everyone's surprise, Roger came home wearing civilian clothes.
8. As if his military uniform no longer fit him.
9. The news traveled quickly.
10. Using the telephone lines and talking over backyard barbecue grills.

Exercise I—Identifying Sentence Fragments

Directions. Study Kuralt's writing. Do you find any sentence fragments in it? Why do you think he writes this way?

Exercise J—Revising Incomplete Sentences

Directions. Five of the following items contain a sentence fragment. In your learning log, number from 1 to 10. Revise the sentences to get rid of the fragments. Leave the others alone.

1. Katrina arrived at the welcoming. Without, however, the present she meant to bring.

2. Listening to patriotic songs, watching videos of the baby, and eating chocolate cake. Everyone tried to remember what Roger had missed.

3. Some people love big parties. Others, like Roger, prefer a quiet family reunion.

4. Some children leave their toys throughout the house. As though they are marking a trail.

5. Roger's son was still quite young. In fact, he was only able to crawl.

6. Trying to catch up on a year's activities takes time. Besides, Roger's family discovered, catching up also takes thought.

7. Feeling light-headed, Roger left the room. Friends and family worried about him.

8. Everything would have been okay. If only Roger had told everyone he had a headache.

9. Going through all the greeting cards. Roger realized he had many friends.

10. Still more greetings came by phone over the next week. Phone bills must have been high!

Final Draft

Prepare a final draft, making revisions and proofreading corrections. Use good form. That means indent each paragraph. Keep neat margins, and add a catchy title.

Peer-editor Activity. Ask a peer to read your paper and check for sentence fragments. Revise as needed.

Peer/Self-editing Chart

Use the following questions to check your final draft.

1. Did I find a good topic?
2. Have I used at least one specific, picture-painting word in every sentence?
3. About what percent of my words are specific?
4. Did I use transitional words and phrases?
5. Have I eliminated fragments or incomplete sentences?
6. What can I do to make my paper more like Kuralt's?

Make any final corrections to your paper before you share it with your audience.

COMPUTER

If you have trouble with sentence fragments, try numbering each of the sentences in your paper. Use the return (or enter) key to set up the sentences like an exercise. Work through the "exercise" item by item, revising as needed. When you finish, delete the numbers and the hard returns to put the sentences back in paragraph form.

HINT

Internet Connection

One way to learn on your own about the workplace is to go to job listing Web sites like Career Path at URL: http://www.CareerPath.com/index.html

It searches employment ads from newspapers from major cities.

Others include:

Intellimatch (including a standardized resume form) at

http://www.intellimatch.com

America's Job Bank (including information about companies) at

http://www.ajb.dni.us

CareerWEB at

http://www.cweb.com

COMPUTER

Many CD-ROM reference works include atlases. You might want to use these as a source for an up-to-date map.

HINT

SHARING

Share your paper in a cooperative group. Then, as a class, make a list of all the topics you wrote about. Beside each topic, explain how you came up with each idea. Then discuss the answers to the following questions:

1. Where did the class find most of its writing ideas?
2. Where else did the class find writing ideas?
3. What was the most unusual idea? Why?
4. What do these answers tell you about finding ideas of your own?

Portfolio Pointers

Put your final draft into your portfolio. Then, on a separate sheet of paper, answer the following questions:

1. What did I learn about finding a topic to write about?
2. As I wrote this piece, what was hardest for me?
3. What did I learn about writing from someone else in my class?
4. How can I use what I learned in my next paper?

Relating Your Writing to the Workplace: Learning on Your Own

Because the workplace constantly changes, you will always need to learn new things. New practices, new technology, and new information demand that you keep up. First, you will have to figure out what it is that you need to know. Then you will have to find the information you need.

How do you prepare for such a workplace?

It is just as Kuralt says: you have to keep your eyes open. You have to make connections. You have to be curious. What if no one had wondered who Roger was? What if they hadn't turned around to go back and find out?

In the workplace, you will need the same kind of open-eyed curiosity. Start developing it now. Take note of your surroundings. Note details. Many jobs require such attention to detail.

With the class or in a small group, make a list of jobs that demand attention to detail.

Check the Atlas

Consult a map of Ohio. Locate five major Ohio airports from which Kuralt might have shipped his film to New York. Cincinnati, Dayton, Cleveland, Columbus, and Toledo are possible choices. About how far is it from these Ohio airports to New York City?

Interdisciplinary Interest Project: The Soldiers' Return from the Vietnam War

Soldiers returning from Vietnam did not get the usual heroes' welcome. Families like Roger's welcomed home their own, but virtually no public parades or ceremonies made a fanfare of their return. Find newspaper and/or magazine articles that tell why there was no fanfare. How did the soldiers feel? Was the lack of welcome justified?

In a small group, make a KWL chart like the one below. It will help you look for information. When you know what you need to find out, divide the search. Each of you should look for specific information.

KWL CHART

Subject		
K What I Know	W What I Want to Know	L What I Learned
1. no big welcome-home parades	1. why no fanfare	1.
	2. what public thought	2.
2. uncle in Vietnam War but haven't heard him talk about it	3. what media said or did	3.
		4.
3.	4. soldiers' reactions	
4.	5.	

Finding Something to Write About

Prepare an article file (a newspaper file, magazine file, or both) in which you list articles about soldiers' reactions to their return from Vietnam. List the name of the publication in which you found each article, along with its date, title, author. You should also include a short summary. If you can, include photocopies of some articles, especially those with pictures.

chapter 2

Keeping

a Reflective Journal

PREWRITING

Visuals

1. "Sparrow Hawk" by Rorii Kiyomasu
2. "Mondrian's Eyeglasses and Pipe" by André Kertész
3. "Drummers of Ede" by John Biggers
4. "Cow's Skull with Calico Roses" by Georgia O'Keeffe
5. "Taos Pueblo, New Mexico" by Ansel Adams

"One of the best things about paintings is their silence—which prompts reflection and random reverie."

Mark Stevens, art critic
Newsweek

Your Viewer's Response

Artists and photographers use pictures the way writers use words. Pictures and words both tell about thoughts. Pick one of the pictures, or choose a picture on your own from a photo album, magazine, or picture file in the library.

Study each picture. If you had been the artist or photographer, what might you have been thinking about when you painted or took it? Write your response in your learning log.

Sparrow Hawk by Rorii Kiyomasu

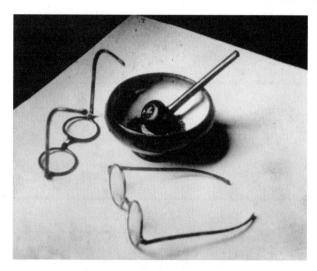

Mondrian's Eyeglasses and Pipe by
André Kertész

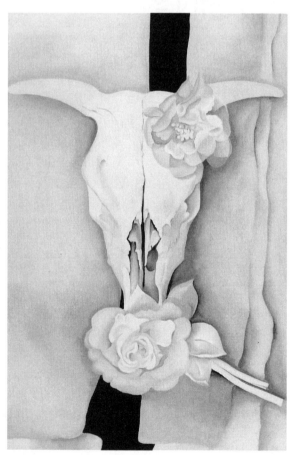

Cow's Skull with Calico Roses
by Georgia O'Keeffe

Taos Pueblo, New Mexico by Ansel Adams

Drummers of Ede
by John Biggers

Reading the Literature

The selection you will read is from a reflective journal. In it, the writer tells what she sees, hears, and remembers. Because she writes in **time order,** she gives details in the order she remembers them. Thus, you can easily follow her thinking—her reflecting.

About the Author

An Inupiaq Eskimo, Rose Atuk Fosdick writes her journal to keep a family history for her son. She has always lived in Nome, Alaska, and she remembers when life was different.

Vocabulary

miniature (MIN I uh chur) adj. very small
mining equipment (MIN ing ee KWIP mint) n. tools and machines used to dig for gold
invisible (in VIZ uh buhl) adj. cannot be seen
impatient (im PAY shunt) adj. upset by slowness
billow (BIL oh) v. puff out
eventually (ee VEN choo uh lee) adv. at last
kuspuk (KOOZ puk) n. woman's long cloth parka

CHICKEN HILL 5/20/87
CAPE NOME 5/22/87
by Rose Atuk Fosdick

from *Raven Tells Stories:*
An Anthology of Alaskan
Native Writing,
edited by *Joseph Bruchac*

Chicken Hill 5/20/87

There is a small hill just outside of Nome which is more like a bump on the ground than a hill. You can hear the birds and you can also hear the powerplant. We're by ourselves, three sisters, and it's good to be free. We cross a stream to get to Chicken Hill. But first we look through brush to see if there are any robins' nests. "Don't breathe on the eggs," Alice says, "the mother won't come back if you do." So we look inside a nest and count the eggs, imagine that the eggs contain miniature robins. Then on to the hill. There's old mining equipment and tunnels and cars to explore. It's never boring and we forget the time, until our stomachs say it's time to eat.

Today I drive by and the hill is covered with dog houses, the three-wheelers zoom up and down on new trails. The birds and flowers are still there but are invisible as we hurry by.

Cape Nome 5/22/87

Below Cape Nome, we would set up berry-picking camp every fall with Grandma. Grandma's tent would be next to ours. She would be the first to wake in the morning impatient to start picking. The soft sound of early morning waves could be heard along with the call of birds heading out to sea. We would wake up to the smell of pancakes and coffee and there would be Mom sitting next to the wood stove cooking breakfast. The sun would be shining, making the white tent twice as bright. The early morning breeze would make the tent door flap open and shut and billow the tent.

Grandma would scold all of us including Mom for being so slow and then giving in to her impatience she would begin the long walk to where the berries were. Eventually we would follow behind her. I can see her walking ahead wearing kuspuk, rubber boots, Eskimo backpack and carrying a walking stick.

Internet Connection

If you have access to the Internet, you may be able to use it to contact active senior citizens. Ask them about their reflections.

Your Reader's Response

Fosdick writes about her childhood. She recalls a favorite play area, a family outing, and a custom she and her sisters had. What events like that can you recall from your own childhood? In your learning log, list 10 memories.

Springboards for Writing

The following activities will help you think of other topics for a reflective journal.

COMPUTER

If you have software that lets you draw, you can create the sunburst on your monitor. Be sure to print out a copy of the sunburst for each group member.

HINT

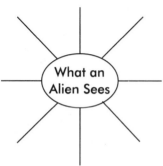

Individual Activity. Interview a senior citizen in your family or community. Ask that person to recall his or her school day, favorite childhood pastime, special play area, or family holiday. Share the stories with your classmates.

Group Activity. With a small group, imagine that an alien from outer space is visiting your class on an ordinary day (or a holiday) and is watching what you do. What would he or she see that would prompt questions? Use a sunburst chart to name these activities. What does the chart suggest for writing topics?

Now Decide

From your Viewer's Response, Reader's Response, or the Springboard activities, pick one topic. It should be a topic similar to Fosdick's. In your learning log, name the topic. Tell why you think it is a good topic for a reflective journal.

Studying the Model: Time Order

Writers must put details in an order that you can follow. Otherwise, you could not make sense of their ideas. Fosdick uses **time order.** Reread her "Chicken Hill" journal entry. See if you can pick out the time order.

Study the following sequence chart. It maps the time order for the first journal entry. In your learning log, list the words that help you see time order.

SEQUENCE CHART FOR "CHICKEN HILL"

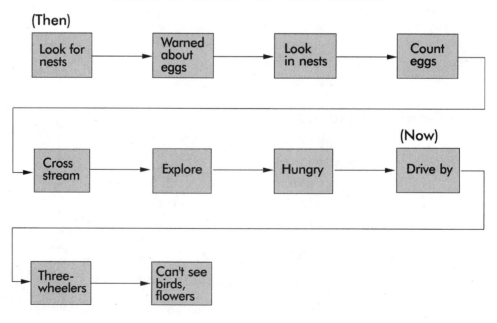

Writing: An Art- and Literature-Based Approach

Mapping Your Writing: Explore with a Sunburst Chart

Use a sunburst chart to explore ideas for your own writing. Write "My Childhood" at the center of your sunburst. On the radiating lines, list events, situations, people, or other memories.

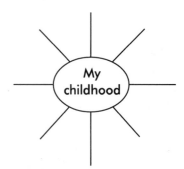

WRITING

Your Assignment

In your learning log, write a reflective journal entry. Like Fosdick, pay attention to daily life. What goes on around you at home? At school? In the neighborhood?

Thinking About the Model

The **time order** that Fosdick uses helps you follow her thoughts. "But first we look through brush," she writes. "Then on to the hill." You can follow what happens first, next, and later.

Use time order in your reflective journal. Use the sequence chart to plan your work.

Writing Process Tip: Focus on Audience

Thinking about your audience helps you know what to write. Fosdick writes her journal for her son because she wants him to know about his culture and heritage.

Think about how you would talk to a three-year-old, to a senior citizen, or to a peer. Your words would be different in each case. Your sentences would be different, too. Even your tone of voice would be different.

Writing is just like talking. As you write, picture your **audience** in your mind's eye. Write as if you were talking to each member of your audience in person.

Now Write

Using your learning log notes and your sequence chart, write your reflective journal entry. Be sure to use words that help readers follow time order.

When you finish your first draft, return to the lesson. You will use Fosdick's writing as a model for revising.

COMPUTER

If you are working on your learning log at the computer, be sure to keep a separate file for reflective journal entries. Your teacher might collect both your disk and your hard copy. Thus, files must be clearly labeled.

Notice that Fosdick names family titles. She writes about her sisters, the robins' mother, Mom, and Grandma.

Two words are capitalized; two are not. Here's the rule:

Capitalize family titles when they are used like names (Mom, Grandma). Do not capitalize them when they have a possesive in front of them (like *her* sisters and *robin's* mother).

REVISING

Checking Model's Map: Time Order

Review the sequence chart on page 26. Then make a sequence chart to plot the time order for "Cape Nome." Do all of the ideas move in time order? Explain.

Use a sequence chart to check the time order in your own writing.

The following exercises will help you understand and use time order.

Exercise A—Arranging Time Order

Directions. In your learning log, number from 1 to 10. Beside each number put the following ideas in time order.

1. baby birds, bird eggs, fledglings, nest
2. new stems, seed pods, buds, flowers
3. mining equipment brought in, claims staked, gold found, gold mines opened
4. mining equipment used, mining equipment bought, mining equipment rusting, mining equipment abandoned
5. buzzer, jump ball, coin toss, points scored
6. Fourth of July, Veterans Day, Thanksgiving, Memorial Day
7. rake leaves, bare trees, autumn colors, dispose of leaves
8. start car, unlock car, back out, find keys, open garage door
9. open box, empty contents, assemble, read assembly instructions, read operating instructions
10. study kinds of software, teach little brother how to use it, choose best one, make purchase, learn to use it

Checking the Links—Words That Show Time Order

Some words help writers show time order. Some of them are listed here:

first	meanwhile	eventually	sometime
next	later	following	soon
then	after	before	earlier
finally	afterward	last	second
eventually	now	over	third
still	while	as	

Sometimes these words are part of a group of words that show time order. For instance,

when	(as in *when the sun went down* . . .)
after	(as in *after school* . . .)
until	(as in *until the first snow falls* . . .)
before	(as in *before school in the morning* . . .)

When one of the time-order words is followed by a noun, the group of words is called a **phrase,** such as *after school* and *before school in the morning.*

When one of the time-order words is followed by a noun and a verb, the group of words is called a clause, such as *when the sun went down* and *until the first snow falls.*

Fosdick uses time-order words, phrases, and clauses. Can you find them? (HINT: There are only a few in "Cape Nome.") Did you find time-order words that are not on the list above? Which ones?

The following exercises give you practice in using time-order words and word groups.

Exercise B—Using Time-order Words

Directions. In your learning log, number from 1 to 10. Read the sentences below. Find a time-order word that makes the meaning clear. Write it in your log. More than one answer can be right. The first one is done for you.

1. Fosdick remembers the hillside filled with brush, birds, and berries. <u>Now,</u> dog houses and three-wheelers cover the hillside.

2. _____ they would climb the hill to explore old mining tunnels and equipment.

3. They played _____ they grew hungry.

4. _____ they ran home to get something to eat.

5. They probably ate quickly and _____ ran back to explore the old cars.

6. Do you think the flowers and birds' nests are _____ there?

7. The first journal entry is dated 5/20/87. _____ Fosdick wrote a second journal entry.

8. In it, she talks about berry picking. Grandma always woke up _____.

9. _____ everyone else was up and ready to go berrying.

10. _____ Grandma was well on her way, everyone else caught up.

Exercise C—Using Time-order Word Groups

Directions. Number your learning log from 1 to 10. Choose a time-order phrase or clause that will connect the ideas. Write it in your log. The first one is done for you.

1. <u>While remembering her childhood,</u> Fosdick lives in the present.

2. _____, Fosdick is writing down what she remembers about her childhood and her family.

3. _____, her son will want to know about his heritage.

4. Her son probably won't be interested _____.

5. _____, Fosdick may be too old to remember the details about her youth.

6. Now, however, her journal makes good reading for others. _____ her son will learn what you already know.

7. Meanwhile, _____, you have a small idea about Eskimo life.

8. _____, you may be inspired to keep a reflective journal for your own family.

9. If so, you can begin now and keep the journal _____.

10. _____, your family will be grateful for your thoughts.

Exercise D—Writing Time Order

Directions. In your learning log, number from 1 to 10. See the pictures on pages 22–23. Complete two sentences about each picture to show time order.

1. After the sparrow hawk was trained, _____.
2. _____ while the hawk groomed itself.
3. At the end of the day, Mondrian _____.
4. When neither pair of glasses helped him read, Mondrian _____.
5. As the drummers of Ede played, _____.
6. Their music finished, the drummers of Ede _____.
7. After seeing the bleached cow's skull in the desert, O'Keeffe, _____.
8. _____ after O'Keeffe added the calico roses.
9. When _____, the Native Americans of Taos Pueblo invite tourists into their village.
10. Having kept their old culture, _____.

Exercise E—Finding Time Order in Your Writing

Directions. Before you wrote your draft, you made a sequence chart for your journal entry. Compare it with your draft. Did you follow time order? Did you use time-order words, phrases, and clauses? Add them as needed.

Peer-editor Activity. Ask a peer to read your paper and suggest at least two more time-order words, phrases, or clauses that you can add.

PROOFREADING

Right Reading: Subject-Verb Agreement

The subject must agree with its verb. For the most part, you will have no trouble with that. In some cases, though, a few rules help. In short, here they are:

1. Words between the subject and its verb sometimes cause errors. For instance,

    A dish of grapes is on the table. (dish is)

    Each of the students is in his seat. (each is)

2. If a sentence has two subjects, use these rules:
   a. If the subjects are joined by *and,* use a plural verb.
      EXAMPLE: Fosdick and her son *live* in Nome.
      Think: [They] live.
      Think: 1 and 1 = 2 (plural)
   b. If the subjects are joined by *or* or *nor* and both subjects are singular, use a singular verb.
      EXAMPLE: Neither Fosdick nor her son *lives* in an igloo.
      Think: [She] lives nor [he] lives.
      Think: 1 nor 1 = 0 (singular)
   c. If the subjects are joined by *or* or *nor* and both subjects are plural, use a plural verb.
      EXAMPLE: The Fosdicks or their relatives rarely *think* about others reading her journal.
      Think: [They] or [they] think
      Think: 2 or 2 = 2 (plural)
   d. If the subjects are joined by *or* or *nor* and one subject is singular and one is plural, make the verb agree with the subject closer to the verb.
      EXAMPLE: Either the Fosdicks or their son *has* the royalty rights to the journal.
      EXAMPLE: Either their son or the Fosdicks *have* the royalty rights to the journal.
      Think: [They] or [he] has. [He] or [They] have.
      Think: 2 or 1 = 1 (singular) 1 or 2 = 2 (plural)
3. If the subject is a pronoun, use these rules.
   e. Some pronouns are always singular: *each, every, one, everyone, anyone, everybody, anybody.*
      EXAMPLE: Everyone *is* in his seat.
      Think: Every[single]one is in his seat.
      EXAMPLE: Anybody in the hallway *is* apt to be in trouble.
      Think: Any[single]body is in trouble.
   f. Some pronouns can be singular or plural: *some, any, all, none,* and *most.*
      EXAMPLE: Some of the sugar *is* on the floor.
      EXAMPLE: Some of the cups *are* broken.

Writing: An Art- and Literature-Based Approach

The following exercise will help you practice subject-verb agreement.

Exercise F—Finding Subject-Verb Agreement

Directions. Find the subject(s) and verb in each of these sentences. Write your answers in your learning log.

1. Fosdick and her sisters play among the old pieces of mining equipment.
2. Neither she nor her sisters have realized the danger.
3. Rusty parts break with little pressure.
4. The equipment and old trucks are left from the gold rush days in the early 1900's.
5. Bankrupt miners have walked away, leaving their equipment to rust.
6. Unfortunately, not everyone has struck gold.
7. Some of the bankrupt miners found other jobs in the area.
8. Perhaps each of them has learned a hard lesson.
9. Today, visitors and residents still see the remains of the mines.
10. Neither rusty trucks nor an abandoned mine makes a safe playground.

Exercise G—Making Subjects and Verbs Agree

Directions. Choose the correct verb. Write your answers in your learning log.

1. Fosdick's son (is/are) likely to be proud of his heritage.
2. Brothers, sisters, and one cousin (makes/make) up the extended family.
3. Her grandparents or an aunt (keeps/keep) Fosdick writing in her journal.
4. Each of them (knows/know) how important heritage is.
5. Some of the Eskimo culture (is/are) well preserved.
6. Fortunately, museums like the Maniilaq Association (was/were) established to preserve the culture.

7. The member villages of the association (is/are) of the northern coastal region.

8. All of the members (is/are) actively preserving the culture.

9. Other villages along the Aleutian Chain (has/have) museums, too.

10. Each of the children there (is/are) part of that rich heritage.

Exercise H—Correcting Subject-Verb Agreement Errors

Directions. Some of these sentences have subject-verb agreement errors. Some are okay. In your learning log, number from 1 to 10. Correct sentences which have errors. Leave the others alone.

1. The kuspuk is a woman's cloth parka.
2. Each of the women wear it as a warm blouse.
3. Since it also has a hood, it doubles as a jacket.
4. The large pocket in the front and a flared skirt gives added warmth.
5. The front pocket or the skirt makes the kuspuk different from most parkas.
6. At the turn of the century, traders brought colorful bags of flour.
7. Since the Inupiaq women didn't use flour, they dumped it and made kuspuks from the flour bags.
8. The cloth dresses was more comfortable than fur in the summer.
9. Either the comfort or the coolness were sure to make the women happy.
10. Everyone in the villages still wear the kuspuk.

Exercise I—Checking Your Work

Directions. With a peer read your reflective journal entry. Highlight the verbs. Does each agree with its subject? Revise as needed.

Final Draft

Prepare a final draft, making revisions and proofreading corrections. Use good form: Indent each paragraph. Keep neat margins. Add a catchy title.

Peer/Self-editing Chart

Use the following questions to check your final draft.

1. Did I choose a good topic?
2. Did I use good specific details?
3. Are my ideas given in time order?
4. Have I used at least one time-order word, one phrase, and one clause?
5. Do all of my verbs agree with their subjects?
6. What can I do to make my journal entry more specific?

Make any final corrections to your journal entry.

SHARING

Generally, reflective journals are not for sharing with large groups. Fosdick, for instance, writes for her son. In your case, share with your classmates how you decided what to write about. Was it something that happened to you? Something you noticed for the first time?

Portfolio Pointers

Put your final draft into your portfolio. Then, on a separate sheet of paper, answer the following questions.

1. What did I learn about finding a topic?
2. As I wrote this journal entry, what was hardest for me?
3. What did a classmate teach me about writing?
4. How can I use what I learned in my next paper?

Relating Your Writing to the Workplace: Planning a Work Day

Most businesspeople follow a time-order schedule. Some schedules are routine. Every day is the same series of tasks. Other schedules vary. Each day puts workers on a different route or task or has them meeting and working with different people.

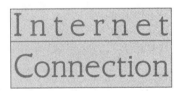

Internet Connection

You can find detailed maps and other geographic details at the following URLs:

Maps at
http://www.cco.caltech.edu/~salmon/maps.html.

CIA WorldFactbook at
http://www.odci.gov/cia/publications/95fact/index.html. (updated annually)

Talk with your parents or other working adults. Ask them about their work schedules. Use the example below to map out a typical workday for one of the people.

Sample Schedule
Thursday, October 4

8:00–8:15	Open mail
8:15–8:30	Answer mail
8:30–9:00	Follow-up phone calls
9:00–9:30	Meet with Marie, Jose, and Wilson
9:30–9:40	Drive to conference center
9:45–11:00	Set up exhibit, including software, advertising, and promotional literature
11:00–11-30	Lunch
11:30–3:00	Work exhibit
3:00–3:15	Break. Check voice mail
3:15–5:30	Work exhibit

Discuss what you learned about work schedules. Did some seem more interesting than others? If so, why?

Check the Atlas

On a map, locate Alaska. Pinpoint Nome, where Fosdick lives. Is Cape Nome identified? If not, can you guess where it is? Where is the Aleutian Chain? Why do you think it's called a chain? What other cities around the world are at the same latitude as Nome? Are there any other cities in the United States that far north?

Interdisciplinary Interest Project: Native Foods in Your Backyard

Rose Atuk Fosdick writes about gathering berries near her home. What native foods grow near *your* school or home? Berries or other fruits? Greens? Roots? Grains or other seeds? Mushrooms? Where do they grow? In full sun? In the shade? In dry areas? In open fields? On vines? Who would have used these native foods for subsistence? Are they still used? How do you know which wild foods are safe to eat?

Consult the local library or horticulturalist. Prepare a list of local wild edibles and illustrate the list with drawings or photographs.

chapter 3

Telling

What You Hear, See, Smell, Taste, and Feel

PREWRITING

Visuals

1. "The Bronco Buster" by Frederic Remington
2. "The Great Wave Off Kanagawa" by Katsushika Hokusai
3. "Shoe Shine Boy" by Elizabeth Catlett
4. "Drive Wheels" By Charles Sheeler
5. "The Piper" by Hughie Lee-Smith

> *"Nothing we use or hear or touch can be expressed in words that equal what is given by the senses."*
> Hannah Arendt, German-born American historian
> *New Yorker*

Your Viewer's Response

Put yourself in one of these paintings. What do you think you would hear, see, smell, taste, and feel?

In your learning log, divide a page into five columns. Label them "Hear," "See," "Smell," "Taste," and "Feel." At the top of the page, name the painting you have picked. Then list as many details as you can in each column.

Compare your lists with those your peers made. Can you add anything to your list?

The Bronco Buster by
Frederic Remington

Shoe Shine Boy by Elizabeth Catlett

The Piper
by Hughie Lee-Smith

The Great Wave Off Kanagawa by Katshushika Hokusai

Drive Wheels by
Charles Sheeler

Reading the Literature

The selection you are about to read shows how one writer uses details that let readers hear, see, smell, taste, and feel. Words that give details about the five senses are called **sensory words.** As you read, watch for the sensory words in this passage.

About the Author

A Japanese-American girl, Yoshiko Uchida (1921–1992) grew up in California. Uchida's youth gave her much to write about, and she writes about it the best way: she tells what she heard, saw, smelled, tasted, and felt. Such details let *you* experience the events, too.

Vocabulary

haze (HAYZ) n. smog

vineyard (VIN yerd) n. a place where grapes grow

reins (RAYNZ) n. strips of leather attached to the bit in a horse's mouth, used by the rider to control the horse

enormous (ee NOR muhs) adj. quite large

Berkeley (BERK lee) city on San Francisco Bay in California

banking (BANGK ing) v. arranging the ashes and fire so it will burn low and long

procedures (proh SEE juhrs) n. ways of doing something

immense (im MENS) adj. very large

Excerpt From

TUB UNDER THE STARS
by Yoshiko Uchida

from *The Invisible Thread*

Oji San waited until the sun had dipped down behind the dusty grapevines and a soft dusky haze settled in the air. Then he announced he was taking us all on a moonlight ride through the vineyards. It was more than we'd ever hoped for.

Keiko took her usual place up front by Oji San, hoping for a brief chance at the reins. Mama and Papa chatted quietly with Oba San, and I lay stretched out in back, looking up at the enormous night sky.

There seemed to be millions and billions of stars up there. More than I'd ever imagined existed in the universe. They seemed brighter and closer than they were in Berkeley. It was as though the entire sky had dropped closer to earth to spread out its full glory right there in front of me.

I listened to the slow *clop-clop* of the mules as they plodded through the fields, probably wondering why they were pulling a wagonload of people in the dark, instead of hauling boxes of grapes to the shed under the hot, dry sun.

I could hear crickets singing and frogs croaking and all the other gentle night sounds of the country. I felt as though I were in another more immense, never-ending world, and wished I could keep riding forever to the ends of the earth.

When we got back to the farm, it was time for an outdoor Japanese bath. Oji San built a fire under a square tin tub filled with water, banking the fire when the water was hot and inserting a wooden float so we wouldn't burn our feet or backsides when we got in.

Oba San hung some sheets on ropes strung around the tub and called out, "*Sah, ofuro!* Come, Kei Chan, Yo Chan. The bath is ready. You girls go first."

Mama gave us careful instructions about proper bathing procedures. "Wash and rinse yourselves outside before you get into the tub," she reminded us. "And keep the water clean."

When we were ready to climb in, I saw steam rising from the water and was afraid I'd be boiled alive. "You go first," I told my sister.

As always, Keiko was fearless. She jumped right in and sank down in the steaming water up to her neck.

"Ooooooh, this feels wonderful!" she said.

I quickly squeezed in next to her, and we let the warm water gurgle up to our chins.

Keiko looked up at the glorious night sky and sighed, "I could stay here forever."

"Where? In the tub?"

"No, silly. In Livingston, of course."

Telling What You Hear, See, Smell, Taste, and Feel

Long after I came home, I remembered Livingston, not as the small dusty farm it was, but as a magical place.

Even now, when I close my eyes, I can see the smiling, sun-browned faces of Oji San and Oba San welcoming us to their farm. I can hear our watery giggles in the steaming outdoor tub, and I can hear the small quiet songs of the creatures in the fields.

But most of all I remember the wagon ride and see again that night sky exploding with stars. It is like a beautiful speckled stone I can take from the pocket of my memory to look at over and over, remembering again the sweet peace of that little farm.

I have written about it in several of my books and stories, and the memory of it even now brings a rush of joy to my heart.

Your Reader's Response

Think about how you would have felt if you had been a part of Uchida's moonlight ride and outdoor Japanese bath. Do you think you would have found it as "magical" as Uchida describes it? Why or why not? Write your response in your learning log.

Springboards for Writing

To find your own topic, chose one or both of the following activities.

Individual Activity. A "magical" or special memory like Uchida's can be happy or sad. It might be of a two-week vacation. Or it might be of one evening, such as the memory Uchida describes. It might be of only a single moment, such as when you were told your parents were getting a divorce.

In your learning log, make a list of at least five memories that are "magical" or special to you. Your memories can come from anywhere: home, school, your old neighborhood. They can involve family, friends, or pets. The pictures at the start of this chapter might even help you think of a special memory.

After you have listed five memories, go back and add two or three details about each.

Group Activity. On a separate sheet of paper, make two lists. In the first, list five special times of the year—such as Valentine's Day—that can trigger a special memory. In the second, list five important places—such as the local ice cream shop—that can trigger a special memory. The pictures at the start of this chapter might also remind you of special times and places. Share your lists with your classmates.

Now Decide

From your individual and/or group work, decide on one memory you are willing to share with others. Write a sentence about it in your learning log. Your sentence may say something like, "My happy/sad memory is of . . . "

Studying the Model: Sensory Words

In "Tub under the Stars," Yoshiko Uchida uses words that tell about what she hears, sees, smells, tastes, and feels. We call these **sensory words.** They refer to the five senses.

For instance, she writes about "dusty grapevines." You can see and smell the dust. She writes about the "slow *clop-clop* of the mules," the "crickets singing and frogs croaking." You can hear them. She writes about "squeezing in" next to her sister in the hot tub and letting "the warm water gurgle up to our chins." You can feel it.

Uchida uses many sensory words. In your learning log or with a peer, make a list of the words that she uses for the five senses. Then study the list. What kinds of words are they? Nouns? Verbs? Adjectives? Adverbs?

Internet Connection

If you have access to the Internet, chat with students in other states or in other parts of the world. To find these students, consult an Internet directory. McKinley Internet Yellow Pages is one such directory. Your local library should have one available.

Ask students on the Net to tell you about a special memory. Do their memories help you remember something special? Share with them in return.

Mapping Your Writing: Think with a Sensory-language Chart

In your learning log, divide a paper into five columns. Label each column for one of the five senses: hear, see, smell, taste, and feel. At the top of the page, name the memory you plan to write about. List sensory words that will help readers share your memory.

SENSORY-LANGUAGE CHART

My Topic: _____

Hear	See	Smell	Taste	Feel

WRITING

Your Assignment

You have decided on a "magical" or special memory in your life. In your learning log, write a first draft about the event. Tell about what you heard, saw, smelled, tasted, and felt. The following activities will help you.

Thinking About the Model

Uchida uses many **sensory words.** Through her words, you see the "smiling, sun-browned faces," hear "our watery giggles," feel "the steaming outdoor tub," and hear the "small quiet songs of the creatures in the fields."

Your sensory-language chart will help you write the way Uchida does.

Uchida also makes sure that every word in the passage leads the reader to the same idea. Every detail shows how much she liked the wagon ride and outdoor bath. Nothing detracts. In other words, the writing shows **unity.**

Writing: An Art- and Literature-Based Approach

Make your own writing do the same. If you write about a happy memory, for instance, make all the details happy.

Writing Process Tip: Deciding on Purpose

Uchida's purpose in "The Tub under the Stars" is to show that she enjoyed a moonlight trip and outdoor bath. You know that she remembers the time fondly and relives it in her mind. As you read, you share her experiences.

When you write, you must decide on your purpose. Then you, too, must use details to help your readers (your audience) share your experiences.

You have chosen a topic. Now, in your learning log, write one sentence that states the purpose of your paper. You may begin with "The purpose of my paper is to . . . " Be sure to include audience.

As you write your paper, think about your purpose.

Now Write

Begin with your topic sentence. Make sure all the details help achieve your purpose and suit the audience.

After you have finished your first draft, return to the lesson. Uchida's writing will serve as a model to help you revise.

REVISING

Checking Model's Map: Unity

Every detail Uchida uses points to the good things about the farm visit. She avoids mentioning bad things, such as bug bites, the searing sun, or the wagon's hard, rough ride.

When every detail supports the writer's purpose, the writing has **unity.** Uchida's story shows unity. Make sure your writing does the same.

The following exercises will help you understand unity.

Exercise A—Unity in Word Groups

Directions. These groups of words lack unity. In each group, one word does not belong with the others. It destroys the unity of the group. In your learning log, number from 1 to 10. Beside each number, write the word that

CAPITALIZATION TIP

Often, the title of a piece names the unifying idea. Written, titles get special treatment. "Tub Under the Stars" is a chapter in Uchida's book *The Invisible Thread.* Note that the main words in both titles are capitalized. Also, note that titles of large works (such as books) are in italics (or underlined), but titles of small works (such as chapters) are in quotation marks.

destroys unity. Explain why. (You might find more than one right way to answer.)

> EXAMPLE: croaking, dusty, clop-clop, singing, giggles
> Word that breaks unity: dusty (Each of the other words names a sound.)

1. mule, frog, cricket, fish, tree
2. sky, stars, moon, sun, comet
3. jacket, shoe, blazer, sport coat, overcoat
4. CD, record, radio, lamp, audio tape
5. pizza, mashed potatoes, hamburger, hot dog, Pepsi
6. Ford, Caprice, Cadillac, Lexus, Jeep
7. keyboard, monitor, disk drive, paper, printer
8. sports, editorial, reporters, comics, advertising
9. broad jump, baseball, relay, pole vault, hurdles
10. linoleum, floor, carpet, tile, rug

Exercise B—Unity in Sentences

Directions. Assume that the following sentences are part of a paragraph. The writer wants to show that she enjoys feeding birds. Like Uchida, she needs to maintain unity. Decide which sentences will fit her purpose and give the paragraph unity.

In your learning log, number from 1 to 10. Mark a plus (+) for sentences that will show unity in the paragraph. Mark a zero (0) for sentences that do not.

1. Birds bring bright colors to the yard: red, blue, yellow, and rose.
2. The birds make messes on the sidewalk and patio.
3. It costs too much to feed them all summer.
4. The more kinds of food I put out—like grain, suet, and fruit—the more kinds of birds I have.
5. In the spring and fall, migrants stop to eat.
6. Part of the fun is in trying to identify all of the birds.
7. I hate to fill feeders when it's cold or raining.
8. When feed gets wet and rots, cleaning is a smelly job.
9. Usually the adult birds bring their young to the feeders.

10. It's fun to see the differences among the male, female, and young of a species.

Exercise C—Write Sentences with Unity

Directions. In your learning log, number from 1 to 10. Each of the sentences below is about one of the pictures on pages 38–39. Write two more sentences for each. Keep the unity.

a. The bronco buster rode rough.
   1. _____
   2. _____
b. Waves nearly hid the boaters.
   3. _____
   4. _____
c. Without shoes of his own, Egrid hustled shoeshine jobs on the street.
d. The noisy old steam engine hissed and spit.
e. Music gave Stanley his only escape.

Exercise D—Unity in Your Writing

Directions. When you finish your first draft, review your purpose. Then read each sentence in your draft. Does every sentence fit the purpose? Revise to get rid of anything that does not.

Peer-editor Activity. Ask a peer to read your draft to check for unity.

Checking the Links: Using Repetition to Make Connections

Look at Uchida's story. You will find words and ideas repeated: *dusty* and *dry*, *ride* and *riding*, *night sky*, and *steam* and *steaming*. With these, she helps you follow and make connections among the ideas.

At the same time, however, you are not always aware that she repeats ideas. That's because she uses words with similar meanings, such as *dusty* and *dry*. She also uses words in different forms, as in *steam* and *steaming*.

Uchida writes, "When we were ready to climb in, I saw steam rising. . . . " Then she says, "[Keiko] jumped right in and sank down in the steaming water. . . . " Next, "I

PUNCTUATION TIP

One way to stress a word is to use an appositive. An appositive renames the noun it follows:

Uchida, *the author of this story*, writes about her childhood in California.

Be sure to set off appositives with commas.

quickly squeezed in next to her, and we let the warm water gurgle up to our chins."

The words *right in* and *squeezed in* echo *climb in*. The word *steaming* echoes *steam*. And the word *warm* expresses the same ideas.

Although Uchida uses similar words to make connections, she does not use the exact same words. Do the same in *your* writing.

The following exercises will help you learn to use repetition to show connections.

Exercise E—Finding Repetition

Directions. Uchida uses repetition to connect ideas. Compare her first three paragraphs with her last three. In your learning log, make a list of the words or ideas Uchida repeats. You should find at least six key words or ideas repeated, such as "dusty grapevines" and "dusky haze."

Exercise F—Repetition with Pronouns

Directions. Pronouns (such as *he, she, it, we,* and *they*) help us repeat without using the same words. Find at least fifteen pronouns in Uchida's writing. In your learning log, list the pronouns. Beside each, name the word or idea to which the pronoun refers.

> EXAMPLE: Uchida writes about the "*clop-clop* of the mules as they plodded through the fields." *They* is a pronoun that repeats the idea *mules*.

Exercise G—Repetition in Your Writing

Directions. Study your first draft. Have you used repetition to connect sentences smoothly for your reader? Have you avoided too much repetition? Have you used pronouns to connect?

In your learning log, make a list of the repeated words and ideas you use. Be sure to include pronouns and the words or ideas they repeat.

Peer-editor Activity. When you have finished Exercise G, ask a peer to check your work.

Exercise H—Sensory Language in Your Writing

Directions. Before you wrote your first draft, you made a sensory-language chart. Compare it with your draft. Did you use at least four of the five senses in your paper? Does almost every sentence include one or more sensory words? Revise as needed to add sensory language.

Peer-editor Activity. Ask a peer to read your paper and suggest at least two more places where you can add sensory words.

PROOFREADING

Right Reading: Noun-Pronoun Agreement and Clear Pronoun Reference

A pronoun agrees in number and gender with the noun to which it refers. Uchida uses nearly all of the pronoun forms: singular and plural; masculine, feminine, and neuter. Here are examples:

1. The girls riding in the wagon with Oji San heard him talking quietly. (*Him* is masculine singular and agrees with the singular noun *grandfather*.)

2. Yoshiko told her sister to test the bath water. (*Her* is feminine singular and agrees with the noun *Yoshiko*.)

3. Oji San loved his nieces and liked treating them to this moonlight ride. (*Them* is plural and agrees with *nieces*.)

4. Talking about the memory, Yoshiko says it is like a speckled stone. (*It* is neuter singular and agrees with *memory*.)

5. Each of the relatives took his turn in the bath. (*His* is singular and agrees with *each*.)

A pronoun also needs a clear reference. Study these examples:

> Unclear: Keiko and Oba San sat up front so she could control the mules.
> (*She* could refer to either *Keiko* or *Oba San*. The reference is unclear.)

COMPUTER

To avoid repeating the same words, use a synonym. Your on-line thesaurus will make this job easy.

HINT

Better: So she might get a chance at the reins, Keiko sat up front with Oba San. (*She* now refers clearly to *Keiko*.)

Use the following exercises to practice using noun-pronoun agreement and clear pronoun references.

Exercise I—Noun-Pronoun Agreement

Directions. Choose the correct pronoun form. Write the answer in your learning log.

1. Yoshiko and Keiko enjoyed (her/their) moonlight ride.
2. Yoshiko wrote about (her/it/them) later in life.
3. Each of the girls had (her/their) own thoughts about the outdoor bath.
4., 5. When Oba San and Oji San used the tub, (she/he/they) followed (her/his/their) cultural heritage.
6. The idea of bathing outdoors seemed strange, but (she/he/it/they) (was/were) part of Yoshiko's fond memory.
7., 8. Yoshiko remembered the big sky, and (she/it/they) recalled that (she/it/they) (was/were) filled with millions and billions of stars.
9. Was it Oba San or Mama who gave (her/their) advice to the girls about bathing?
10. After Oji San heated the bath water, (he/it/they) banked the fire.

Exercise J—Clear Reference

Directions. In your learning log, rewrite the following sentences so that all pronouns have a clear reference.

1. Mama and Oba San used her sheets to give privacy for the bath.
2. When Yoshiko and Keiko tested the water, she said it felt great.
3. As Yoshiko and Keiko rode through the vineyard, its wheels made ruts in the dirt.

Writing: An Art- and Literature-Based Approach

4. The mules pulled it along at a steady *clop-clop* pace.
5. Oji San and Oba San welcomed them to their farm.

Exercise K—Reading Your Writing

Directions. Reread your draft to check for the correct use of pronouns. Have you made each pronoun agree with the noun to which it refers? Does each pronoun have a clear reference?

Peer-editor Activity. Ask a peer to proofread your paper for correct pronouns and clear references.

Final Draft

Prepare a final draft, making revisions and proofreading corrections. Use good form. Add a title.

Peer/Self-editing Chart

Use the following questions to check your final draft.

1. Have I used at least four of the five senses in my paper: hear, see, smell, taste, and feel?
2. Have I used good sensory words that let the reader share my experience?
3. About what percent of my words are sensory words?
4. Does my paper have unity?
5. Have I used good connecting words and ideas?
6. Have I used pronouns correctly?
7. What can I do to make my paper more like Uchida's?

Make final corrections to your description before you share it with your audience.

SHARING

Read or listen to each other's work. As a class, create a sensory-language chart for your papers. Then discuss the answers to these questions:

1. Which of the five senses was easiest to include? Why?
2. Which was the hardest? Why?
3. About what percent of the class's words are sensory words? What does this say about your writing?

COMPUTER

Computer language is filled with technical terms. Look at a computer manual. What sensory words are used? What conclusions can you reach about computer language?

HINT

Portfolio Pointers

Put your final draft into your portfolio. Then, on a separate sheet of paper, answer the following questions:

1. What did I learn about my writing from this assignment?
2. Which part of the process was hardest for me? Why?
3. If I had it to do over, what would I do differently?

Relating Your Writing to the Workplace: Using Technical Language

Sensory language tells readers what you hear, see, smell, taste, and feel. It is essential for sharing experiences.

In the workplace, however, the job determines the language you use. For instance, your job may be to write instructions for programming a VCR. No one cares what you smell, taste, or feel. Instead, you must use technical words that match the VCR. In short, language matches the purpose.

Bring to class a piece of technical writing such as a brochure or manual. With a peer, list the technical words from one paragraph. Are there any sensory words? If so, to which senses do they appeal? Discuss what you find.

Check the Atlas

On a United States map, locate California, where the vineyards grow. Find Berkeley, where the girls live. Then find Livingston, where their grandparents' farm is. How far is the girls' home from the farm?

Interdisciplinary Interest Project: Japanese Internment Camps in the US during World War II

As an American citizen, Yoshiko Uchida spent a year with her parents and sister in a concentration camp in Topaz, Utah. She often wrote about her life there.

Research the topic of Japanese-American concentration camps during World War II. Explore questions such as these: Why were American citizens put into camps? How did they live? What happened to their property and possessions while they were there? What happened when they got out? How did the public feel about the camps? Why? How do people feel today? Why? In an oral report, share what you find with your class.

chapter 4

Describing

a Place You Like

PREWRITING

Visuals

1. "Paris Street: Rainy Day" by Gustave Caillebotte
2. "Cafe Express" by Richard Estes
3. "Woods and Valleys of Yu-shan" by Ni Tsan
4. "Snow in Santa Fe" by Paul Lantz
5. "Red Leaves" by Elizabeth Catlett

"The West is color. . . . Its colors are animal rather than vegetable, the colors of earth and sunlight and ripeness."
Jessamyn West, author "The West—A Place to Hang Your Dreams"

Your Viewer's Response

The pictures on the following pages are of places the artists like. Pick one of the pictures, or pick a place *you* like: a park, neighborhood, vacation spot, restaurant, school, or room. You might also choose a snowy forest, hot desert, spring meadow, sandy beach, or busy street.

What makes you like a certain place? Is it the activities connected with it? The people? The memories? The season? In your learning log, make two columns. In the left column list 3 or 4 places you like. In the right column list words that tell why you like each place.

Paris Street: Rainy Day by Gustave Caillebotte

Cafe Express
by Richard Estes

Woods and Valleys of Yu-shan
by Ni Tsan

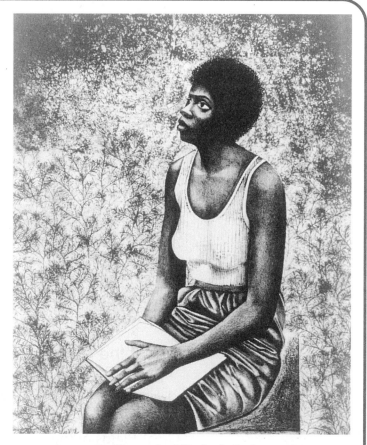

Red Leaves by Elizabeth Catlett

Snow in Santa Fe by Paul Lantz

EXAMPLE:

Kitchen at home smells good

lots of activity—everybody there

computer on corner desk

people come and go through back door

play board games at table

Reading the Literature

In this selection, the writer describes the place where he grew up. To tell you what it was like, he uses comparisons. For instance, he says, "In summer the prairie is an anvil's edge," and grasshoppers were "popping up like corn." Called **similes and metaphors,** these comparisons help you "see" one of Momaday's favorite places. Watch for them as you read.

About the Author

Born to the Kiowa Indians, N. Scott Momaday (1934–) remembers what he learned from his grandmother. In this selection, he celebrates his love and respect for her and the Great Plains of their people.

Vocabulary

knoll (NOL) n. low hill

tornadic (tor NAD ik) adj. like terrible winds of a tornado

anvil (AN vuhl) n. a steel block used by a blacksmith to hammer metal to shape

linear (LIN ee er) adj. growing in a line

foliage (FOH li ij) n. leaves

writhe (RITH) v. twist and turn

aspect (AS pekt) n. the way something looks

isolate (I soh layt) adj. set apart, alone

proportion (pro POR shuhn) n. size of one thing compared to another

infirm (in FERM) adj. weak and feeble from old age

wake (WAYK) n. a watch over a dead body

mourning (MORN ing) n. grief over loss of loved one

eternal (ee TER nuhl) adj. everlasting

purled (PERLD) v. moved in eddies; swirled

hied (HID) v. hurried

Excerpt From

THE WAY TO RAINY MOUNTAIN
by N. Scott Momaday

A single knoll rises out of the plain in Oklahoma, north and west of the Wichita Range. For my people, the Kiowas, it is an old landmark, and they gave it the name Rainy Mountain. The hardest weather in the world is there. Winter brings blizzards, hot tornadic winds arise in the spring, and in summer the prairie is an anvil's edge. The grass turns brittle and brown, and it cracks beneath your feet. There are green belts along the rivers and creeks, linear groves of hickory and pecan, willow and witch hazel. At a distance in July or August the steaming foliage seems almost to writhe in fire. Great green and yellow grasshoppers are everywhere in the tall grass, popping up like corn to sting the flesh, and tortoises crawl about on the red earth, going nowhere in the plenty of time. Loneliness is an aspect of the land. All things in the plain are isolate; there is no confusion of objects in the eye, but *one* hill or *one* tree or *one* man. To look upon that landscape in the early morning, with the sun at your back, is to lose the sense of proportion. Your imagination comes to life, and this, you think, is where Creation was begun.

I returned to Rainy Mountain in July. My grandmother had died in the spring, and I wanted to be at her grave. She had lived to be very old and at last infirm. Her only living daughter was with her when she died, and I was told that in death her face was that of a child.

Now there is a funeral silence in the rooms, the endless wake of some final word. The walls have closed in upon my grandmother's house. When I returned to it in mourning, I saw for the first time in my life how small it was. It was late at night, and there was a white moon, nearly full. I sat for a long time on the stone steps by the kitchen door. From there I could see out across the land; I could see the long row of trees by the creek, the low light upon the rolling plains, and the stars of the Big Dipper. Once I looked at the moon and caught sight of a strange thing. A cricket had perched upon the handrail, only a few inches away from me. My line of vision was such that the creature filled the moon like a fossil. It had gone there, I thought, to live and die, for there, of all places, was its small definition made whole and eternal. A warm wind rose up and purled like the longing within me.

The next morning I awoke at dawn and went out on the dirt road to Rainy Mountain. It was already hot, and the grasshoppers began to fill the air. Still, it was early in the morning, and the birds sang out of the shadows. The long yellow grass on the mountain shone in the bright light, and a scissortail hied above the land. There, where it ought to be, at the end of a long and legendary way, was my grandmother's grave. Here and there on the dark stones were ancestral names. Looking back once, I saw the mountain and came away.

Your Reader's Response

N. Scott Momaday really likes the place in which he grew up. Compare it with a place in which you grew up. What do you like best about the place in which you grew up? Why? Write your response in your learning log.

Springboards for Writing

The following activities will help you think of writing ideas.

Individual Activity. Look at the log notes you wrote in response to the art and literature. Are some of the places you like more interesting than others? Pick two and then look at the list of reasons you like them. Picture each place in your mind. Draw a sketch of each in your learning log. Then, beside each sketch, list several more details explaining why you like these two places.

Group Activity. With two or three peers, look again at the pictures on pages 54–55. As a group, list five places that each of the pictures reminds you of. Narrow the list to a total of five. Write the name of each place in the middle of a sunburst chart. On each line write a reason that someone in the group likes the place.

As a class, share your sunburst charts.

SUNBURST CHART

Name of Place

Writing: An Art- and Literature-Based Approach

Now Decide

From your Viewer's Response, Reader's Response, or the activities above, pick one topic you would most like to write about. In your learning log, write two sentences about your topic. First, tell what place you find interesting. Second, name four or five reasons you find it interesting.

Studying the Model: Word Pictures in Similes and Metaphors

As you learned in Chapter 1, specific details paint pictures. Writers like Momaday make the pictures more interesting by using details that compare. To say that grasshoppers are jumping like popcorn paints a vivid picture. The comparison is called a **simile** if it uses the words *like* or *as*: grasshoppers are "popping up *like* corn."

Momaday makes other comparisons, too. He writes that the "prairie is an anvil's edge," and there are "green belts along the rivers and creeks." These are called **metaphors.** One thing is described as another without the use of the words *like* or *as*.

Check the rest of Momaday's work. What other similes or metaphors can you find? List them in your learning log.

Mapping Your Writing: Try Comparisons with a Sameness Chart

Make a list of five nouns. Find a partner. Put one noun from each of your lists on a sameness chart. For instance, maybe you had "brother" on your list and your partner had "bear." Work together to list qualities that are the same for both nouns.

SAMENESS CHART

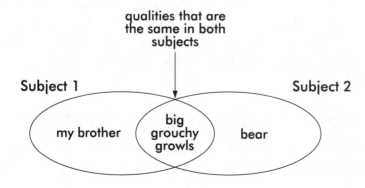

Finally, write a sentence using the comparison in a simile or metaphor. Your sentence might read, "My bear of a brother growls and snarls at everyone." If the words were "potato" and "firecracker," your sentence might read, "Eating the potato, smothered with peppers and hot salsa, was like eating a firecracker."

Do the same with one more pair of nouns. Share your sentences with your classmates.

Now look for comparisons for your own topic. Pick three details from your learning log entries. In your log, draw a sameness chart for each. What comparisons will help you write similes or metaphors?

WRITING

Your Assignment

Choose a place you like and describe it. Write the description so that others will like it, too. Use comparisons in your description, like the similes and metaphors that Momaday uses. The following activities will help you write.

Thinking About the Model

Momaday makes comparisons with **similes and metaphors.** You have made sameness charts to do the same.

Notice, too, that Momaday arranges his words in order to help you follow them in your mind's eye. He tells about winter's blizzards, then spring's hot winds, and finally summer's edge. Thus, he moves through the seasons, following the time order that you learned about in Chapter 2. Momaday also uses another kind of order. He writes first about the distant mountain, then about the nearer trees along the river, and finally about the close-up grasshoppers and turtles. That's called **space order.**

As you write, try to follow Momaday's model.

Writing Process Tip: Finding Your "Little Topic"

Beginning writers often try to write about too much at once. Look at the photograph titled "Red Leaves" on page

55. It represents a "little topic." Instead of showing the whole hillside of autumn trees or even a whole tree, the photographer chose only a few leaves.

Think about the place you like and want to describe. It might be something that is already little, such as your room. In that case you already have a good topic.

What if your topic is something big, such as a park? If it's that big, you must narrow your topic, as the photographer did. Then you can focus on just a small part. That is your "little topic."

In your learning log, name your **little topic** now.

Hint: Maybe the comparisons you wrote on the sameness chart (page 59) will help you find a little topic.

Next, decide on your audience and purpose. Make a note of both in your learning log. (If needed, review the writing-process tips in Chapters 2 and 3.)

Finally, write a topic sentence that names the little topic and gives a clue about it. (If needed, review the writing-process tip in Chapter 1.)

Now Write

Using your sameness charts, your log notes, and the topic sentence you wrote above, write your first draft. Put it in your learning log or use a computer.

When you finish your first draft, return to the lesson. Use Momaday's writing as a model for revising.

REVISING

Checking Model's Map: Space Order

In places, Momaday uses time order. (You learned about that in Chapter 2.) For instance, he writes about winter, then spring, then summer. In the last paragraph he moves from late night, to early morning, to late morning.

Along with time order, Momaday also uses space order. Space order can follow several paths:

left to right, right to left
top to bottom, bottom to top
near to far, far to near

In his first paragraph, Momaday follows the far-to-near path. For instance, he writes first about the distant Rainy Mountain. Next, he writes about the river, which is somewhat closer. Finally, he writes about the nearby tall grass, with its grasshoppers and tortoises. He paints the picture from far away to close up.

Use a space-order map to plot the space order in Momaday's next-to-last paragraph. The first paragraph is plotted below. Use it as a model.

SPACE-ORDER MAP

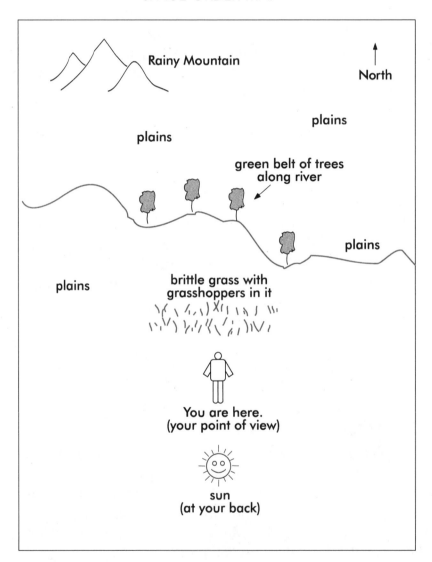

Use the following exercise to practice identifying space order.

Writing: An Art- and Literature-Based Approach

Exercise A—Identifying Logical Space Order

Directions. In your learning log, number from 1 to 10. Study the groups of words below. In parentheses, you are told where you are standing. This is your *point of view*. You are also told the order, such as *near to far* or *right to left*. See if the words are in the correct space order from your point of view. Write "okay" if they are correct. If they are incorrect, change them.

> EXAMPLE: (on the sidewalk, near to far) curb, parked cars, moving cars, center line
>
> ANSWER: Okay

1. (in the street, near to far) sidewalk, street, hotel, beach
2. (facing the flag, left to right) field of blue, 50 white stars, red and white stripes
3. (in the stands at a football game, top to bottom) players, cheerleaders, hot-dog vendor, press box
4. (at computer keyboard, bottom to top) disk drive, monitor, keyboard overlay for commands, keyboard
5. (in front of movie theater ticket window, far to near) lighted marquee, advertisements for what's playing, ticket booth, teller window
6. (in front of apartment building, near to far) steps, roof, door, seven floors of windows
7. (looking at front page of newspaper, top to bottom) photo, banner, main headline, photo caption
8. (from an airplane, near to far) seat belt, wing, clouds, ground features
9. (from diving platform, far to near) water, toes, diving board, fingers
10. (from inside the jack-o'-lantern, near to far) warm and cozy room, inch-thick walls, tough orange skin, cold vast night

COMPUTER

If you need to revise, use the block or select command to move a body of text into better space order. A block move is usually made through the Edit menu with highlighted text.

HINT

Exercise B—Naming Space Order

Directions. See the pictures on pages 54–55. In your learning log, list five details from each picture. Put the details in space order. Name the specific space order.

Exercise C—Revising Your Writing for Space Order

Directions. Review your first draft. Can you find space order? Do the details move logically

—from left to right or right to left?
—from near to far or far to near?
—from top to bottom or bottom to top?

Can you find a place where space order would help your reader? Revise as needed.

Peer-editor Activity. Ask a peer to read your draft for space order.

Checking the Links: Words to Show Space Order

Certain words and word groups show order in space. Momaday uses words such as *at a distance, from there, out, across,* and *only a few inches away* to show space. Many other words or word groups also show space. Here are a few:

next to	below	nearby
between	above	beyond
beside	under	beneath
farther	farthest	across from
nearer	nearest	up from there
to the left of	close by	down from there
right of that	closest	lower
higher	through	in front of
facing	behind	north
south	east	west

The following exercises will help you use good links to show space order.

Exercise D—Identifying Words That Show Space Order

Directions. In your learning log, number from 1 to 10. Read the following sentences and identify the words that show space order. Write them in your log.

1. In front of me, well off in the distance, lay Rainy Mountain.

2. The morning mist settled in the valley between me and the mountain.

3. High up, a hawk soared on the wind.

4. Closer, in the river trees, crows cawed at the morning sun.

5. Nearby finches and sparrows chirped and twittered.

6. All else was silent, but busy—like the spider spinning its web inches from my right shoulder.

7. Across my lap lay a cat, tail hanging down my thigh, ears cocked, idly watching the spider above.

8. My feet, propped on the porch rail in front, shaped a V through which I studied the distant mist.

9. Beyond the mist, where it filled over the generations, lay the cemetery.

10. Somewhere inside its walls lay my grandmother.

Exercise E—Choosing Words to Identify Space Order

Directions. In your learning log, number from 1 to 10. For each blank, find a word or group of words that shows logical space order. Write the word or phrase in your log.

1. _____ in the tall grass, tortoises crawled heedless of time.

2. The red clay _____ painted their toes and tails rust.

3. As the tortoises crawled _____, they disappeared in the dry, broken grasses.

4. _____, parting grasses marked the otherwise unseen creatures' paths.

5. At that moment a stiff breeze rustled leaves _____.

6. A tumbleweed skittered _____ and against the fence.

7. _____ the fence was lined with wind-blown drift—weeds, paper, and plastic bags.

8. Off to the right stood the house, and off _____ was nothing but space.

9. Features stood alone _____: one man, one tree, one fence row.

10. But _____ nothing but the grasshoppers moved.

Exercise F—Similes and Metaphors: Looking for Comparisons in Your Writing

Directions. Before you wrote your first draft, you made three sameness charts of comparisons you might use. Compare them with your draft. Did you use the comparisons as similes or metaphors? Can you add others? Make revisions as needed.

Peer-editor Activity. Ask a peer to read your paper and suggest at least one more place to add a simile or metaphor.

PROOFREADING

Right Reading: Possessive Forms of Nouns and Pronouns

Momaday writes about the *anvil's edge,* his *grandmother's house,* and his *grandmother's grave.* Referring to the cricket, he writes of *its small definition.* In each case, Momaday uses a possessive form.

The possessive form shows ownership. Nouns need an apostrophe to show ownership; pronouns do not. Study these examples:

Big Dipper's stars	its stars
Momaday's home	his home
ancestors' graves	their graves

Remember two rules:

1. When a noun does **not** end in *-s*, add an apostrophe and an *s*.
   - EXAMPLE: the house of one grandmother
   - Thus: the grandmother's house
2. When a noun ends in *-s*, add an apostrophe.
   - EXAMPLE: the graves of twenty ancestors
   - Thus: twenty ancestors' graves

The following exercises will help you identify the correct form of possessive nouns and pronouns.

Exercise G—Writing Possessive Nouns and Pronouns

Directions. In your learning log, write the possessive form of the underlined words.

1. <u>Momaday</u> grandmother died in the spring.
2. <u>He</u> aunt was there, but Momaday was not.
3. When Momaday returned in the summer, the <u>summer</u> heat made everything dry and brittle.
4. Even the <u>tortoises</u> shells looked red from the dust.
5. The <u>grasshoppers</u> habit of jumping reminded Momaday of popping corn without a lid for the pan.
6. As far as the grasshoppers were concerned, the grass was <u>they.</u>
7. Can you imagine the <u>children</u> surprise when they learn that yellow grasshoppers sting?
8. The <u>land</u> main feature is loneliness.
9. <u>It</u> loneliness brings joy to Momaday.
10. It's <u>anybody</u> guess what bitterness winter may bring to the Great Plains.

Exercise H—Distinguishing Between Contractions and Possessives

Directions. In Chapter 2, you studied contractions. Possessive forms and contractions both use apostrophes. Knowing the difference will solve problems later. Review the rules in Chapter 2. Then do this exercise.

Remember:

A **contraction** has a letter or letters missing. If you can't (cannot) find a letter or letters missing, it's (it is) not a contraction.

A **possessive** shows ownership. If you can't put the word in an "of" phrase, it isn't possessive: Momaday's grandmother = grandmother of Momaday.

In your learning log, identify the underlined word as a possessive form or a contraction. Most sentences have more than one word underlined. If a word is a contraction, tell what two words are contracted.

Describing a Place You Like

1. His longing to visit his ancestors' graves points to Momaday's roots.
2. Although he couldn't be with his grandmother at her death, he knows her spirit isn't far away.
3. It's certain that the Kiowa's culture is a fascinating story.
4. Momaday's writing about their culture means they're going to be understood by more people.
5. How's Rainy Mountain similar to the place you like?
6. Isn't the Wichita Mountains' geography part of what makes western Oklahoma beautiful?
7. Can't your favorite place be compared with his?
8. There you'll find part of what the Kiowas call their home.
9. The Kiowas were hunters whose language doesn't fit any other tribe's pattern.
10. The sun's course across the sky is their calendar.

Peer-editor Activity. With a peer, proofread your paper. Check for possessives and contractions. Revise as needed.

Final Draft

Prepare a final draft, making revisions and proofreading corrections. Use good form. Add a catchy title.

Peer/Self-editing Chart

Check your final draft by asking yourself the following questions:

1. Did I choose a good "little" topic?
2. Did I have a good topic sentence?
3. Did I write to my audience?
4. Did I meet my purpose?
5. Have I used at least one specific, picture-painting word in every sentence?
6. Did I make comparisons (at least one simile and one metaphor)?
7. Did I use good space order?
8. Did I use words to help my reader follow the space order?

9. Did I use possessive forms correctly?
10. What can I do to make my paper more like Momaday's?

Make final corrections in your paper before you share it with your audience.

COMPUTER

Your CD-ROM reference materials may include a detailed map of Oklahoma. If so, you can print a copy for posting on the bulletin board.

HINT

SHARING

As a class, make a list of the places you have written about. Group the places. For instance: Places at Home, Places Near Our School, Places Outside the State, and so on. Choose one paper that represents each group. Ask the author or someone else to read aloud each representative work.

Portfolio Pointers

Put your final draft into your portfolio. Then, on a separate sheet of paper, answer the following questions:

1. What did I learn about using similes and metaphors?
2. As I wrote, what was hardest for me?
3. What did a classmate teach me about writing?
4. How can I use my knowledge about space order in other classes?

Relating Your Writing to the Workplace: Making Complex Ideas Simple

In *The Way to Rainy Mountain*, N. Scott Momaday faced the difficult job of explaining to readers why Rainy Mountain is so important to him. Since most of us have never seen Rainy Mountain, he needed to make a complex idea simple.

In the workplace, the refrigerator repairperson faces the same task. She must explain to the customer what is wrong with the refrigerator and how she will repair it. Because most of us have little technical knowledge of refrigeration, we need easy-to-follow explanations about the complex ideas. You will need to do the same in your own job.

Choose a topic that you know something about, such as how a piece of computer software works, how to care for

a pet snake, or how to make spaghetti. Explain the topic to a five-year-old child.

Check the Atlas

On a map of the United States, locate the Wichita Range in southwestern Oklahoma, near the city of Lawton. Put a pin in the map there. From what Momaday says, what do you know about the area? What is it like in July? In January?

Elsewhere in *The Way to Rainy Mountain*, Momaday says the Kiowas once "controlled the open range from the Smoky Hill River to the Red, from the headwaters of the Canadian to the fork of the Arkansas and Cimarron." Locate that area on the map. Shade it in yellow.

Momaday's ancestors were mountain people from western Montana. They migrated south and east through Yellowstone. Locate the migration area on the map. Shade it in pink.

Finally, mark your hometown. Figure the distance between your home and Rainy Mountain. Is it closer than the Montana mountains are to Rainy Mountain?

Interdisciplinary Interest Project: Learning About the Kiowas

The Kiowa Indians have an interesting history. Using clues from Momaday's writing, research the background of the culture. In fact, some students may want to read the rest of Momaday's book, *The Way to Rainy Mountain*. (It's quite short.)

To be efficient, divide the research so that some students search for geographic moves, others check cultural traditions, others learn about modern Kiowas, and so on. Make a KWL chart to guide your research.

When you finish the research, complete the KWL chart and share your findings with the class.

chapter 5

Telling

About Someone You Know

PREWRITING

Visuals

1. "Ma Biggers Quilting" by John Biggers
2. "Niño del Mezquital" by Elizabeth Catlett
3. "Alabama Cotton Tenant Farmer's Wife, 1936" by Walker Evans
4. "Profile in Blue" by Ron Adams
5. "Sea Boots" by Andrew Wyeth

"The analysis of character is the highest human entertainment."

Isaac Bashevis Singer, novelist
The New York Times

Your Viewer's response

Study the pictures on pages 72–73. Whom do they make you think of? In your learning log, number from 1 to 5. Beside each number, name someone that each picture makes you think of.

> EXAMPLES: my sister
>
> lady down the street
>
> Mrs. Kastilette

Reading the Literature

This selection tells about a woman named Miss Lottie. As you read, watch how the author begins each sentence a different way. The **sentence variety** adds reader interest.

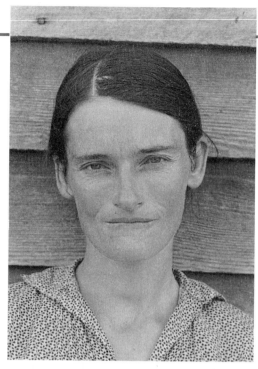

Alabama Cotton Tenant Farmer's Wife, 1936 by Walker Evans

Ma Biggers Quilting by John Biggers

Niño del Mezquital by Elizabeth Catlett

Profile in Blue by Ron Adams

Sea Boots by Andrew Wyeth

About the Author

Although Eugenia W. Collier (1928–) holds degrees from big-name universities, she is most happy about her short-story writing. As an African American, she writes stories that portray powerful black women.

Vocabulary

frame (FRAYM) n. bone structure

stoicism (STOH i siz uhm) n. lack of emotion

intruders (in TROO derz) n. people who visit without being invited

interaction (in ter AK shun) n. working with one another

exploits (EKS ployts) n. brave or remarkable acts

sophisticated (suh FIS tuh kat id) adj. worldly wise

reinforce (ree in FAWRS) v. strengthen

decay (dee KAY) n. rottenness

passionate (PASH uh nit) adj. showing strong feelings

cultivating (KUL tuh vayt ing) v. breaking up the soil around plants to get rid of weeds

perverse (per VERS) adj. wrong, wicked

vigor (VIG er) n. active, healthy force

intimidated (in TIM uh dat id) v. made afraid

cropped (KRAHPT) adj. cut short

reveling (REV uhl ing) n. taking delight in

Excerpt From

M A R I G O L D S

by Eugenia W. Collier

Our real fun and our real fear were found in Miss Lottie herself. Miss Lottie seemed to be at least a hundred years old. Her big frame still held traces of the tall, powerful woman she must have been in youth, although it was now bent and drawn. Her smooth skin was a dark reddish-brown, and her face had Indian-like features and the stern stoicism that one associates with Indian faces. Miss Lottie didn't like intruders either, especially children. She never left her yard, and nobody ever visited her. We never knew how she managed those necessities which depend on human interaction—how she ate, for example, or even whether she ate. When we were tiny children, we thought Miss Lottie was a witch and we made up tales, that we half believed ourselves, about her exploits. We were far too sophisticated now, of course, to believe the witch-nonsense. But old fears have a way of clinging like cobwebs, and so when we sighted the tumble-down shack, we had to stop to reinforce our nerves.

"Look, there she is," I whispered, forgetting that Miss Lottie could not possibly have heard me from that distance. "She's fooling with them crazy flowers."

"Yeh, look at 'er."

Miss Lottie's marigolds were perhaps the strangest part of the picture. Certainly they did not fit in with the crumbling decay of the rest of her yard. Beyond the dusty brown yard, in front of the sorry gray house, rose suddenly and shockingly a dazzling strip of bright blossoms, clumped together in enormous mounds, warm and passionate and sungolden. The old black witch-woman worked on them all summer, every summer, down on her creaky knees, weeding and cultivating and arranging, while the house crumbled and John Burke rocked. For some perverse reason, we children hated those marigolds. They interfered with the perfect ugliness of the place; they were too beautiful; they said too much that we could not understand; they did not make sense. There was something in the vigor with which the old woman destroyed the weeds that intimidated us. It should have been a comical sight—the old woman with the man's hat on her cropped white head, leaning over the bright mounds, her big backside in the air—but it wasn't comical, it was something we could not name. We had to annoy her by whizzing a pebble into her flowers or by yelling a dirty word, then dancing away from her rage, revelling in our youth and mocking her age.

Your Reader's Response

Think about someone older whom you knew as a child. How did you feel about this person then? Have your feelings changed? In your learning log, write your thoughts.

COMPUTER

You can find portraits at the keyboard. CD-ROM reference works usually include photos with biographies and other articles. The *Reader's Guide to Periodical Literature* CD-ROM index will mention whether or not the articles include portraits. Other sources may be available if your computer is networked or if you can connect to a database.

When you find a picture you want to use, download it and print it to share with your class.

HINT

Telling About Someone You Know

Springboards for Writing

These activities will help you think of writing ideas.

Individual Activity. Whom does Miss Lottie remind you of? A neighbor? A relative? Someone you saw just once? Make a six-line character pyramid. Use this guide:

1. In one word, name or identify the person (example: "Lottie").
2. In two words, tell where you usually saw this person (example: "her yard").
3. In three words, describe his or her appearance (example: "old, tall, strong").
4. In four words, describe his or her main characteristics (example: "loves marigolds/great gardener").
5. In five words, name a few other characteristics (example: "annoyed by children, kept working").
6. In six words, tell how you felt toward him or her (example: "knew better but pestered her anyway").

CHARACTER PYRAMID

1. _Lottie_

2. _her_ _yard_

3. _old,_ _tall,_ _strong_

4. _loves_ _marigolds,_ _great_ _gardener_

5. _annoyed_ _by_ _children,_ _kept_ _working_

6. _knew_ _better_ _but_ _pestered_ _her_ _anyway_

Writing: An Art- and Literature-Based Approach

Group Activity. Review the pictures at the beginning of this chapter. With a peer, look for other pictures in newspapers and magazines that show people in many walks of life. Photocopy the five best; post them on a bulletin board. When all of the groups have posted their best, choose one that reminds you of someone you know. Complete a character pyramid for that person.

Now Decide

From your Viewer's Response, Reader's Response, or the activities above, pick one person you would most like to write about. In your learning log, write one sentence about that person. Model your sentence after Eugenia Collier's:

> "Our real fun and our real fear were found in Miss Lottie herself." The words *fun* and *fear* give clues as to how the narrator feels about the character. Include at least one clue in your own topic sentence.

Next, decide on your purpose and audience. Name them in your learning log.

Studying the Model: Sentence Variety; Sentence Beginnings

Eugenia Collier's story about Miss Lottie is a favorite of many people. In part, that is because it reads like music. There are ups and downs, loud parts and soft, rhythm and broken rhythm. If you read the piece aloud, you can hear the music.

The music springs from Collier's **sentence variety.** You can vary sentences by length, type, and beginnings. Collier uses all three; but for now, look at her **sentence beginnings.**

Inexperienced writers often start all sentences the same way—with the subject. Collier, though, begins with other word groups as well. Compare these sentences:

Her big frame still held traces . . .	(adjective)
Her smooth skin was . . .	(adjective)
Miss Lottie didn't like . . .	(subject)
When we were tiny children, we thought . . .	(clause)
Look, there she is . . .	(verb)
Yeh, look at 'er . . .	(linking word)
Miss Lottie's marigolds were . . .	(adjective)

Certain software applications will quickly create graphs, charts, and tables. As you compile the information about Collier's sentence beginnings, input the data and try different formats. Choose the chart, table, or graph that best shows her sentence variety.

Print a hard copy and share it with the class.

HINT

Certainly they did not fit . . .   (linking word)
Beyond the . . . yard, in front of the . . .
    house, rose . . . a dazzling strip . . .   (two phrases)

With the rest of the class, decide how each sentence begins. Make a chart to show how many sentences begin with a subject, verb, linking word, phrase, or clause.

Mapping Your Writing: Think with a Character Chart

In your learning log, make a character chart. Here's how:

Draw a stick figure. Then draw arrows from the head, eyes, ears, mouth, heart, hands, and feet. In thought bubbles, write something your character thinks, sees, hears, says, feels, or does. Then tell where he or she goes.

CHARACTER CHART

Character's Name or Identity: _____

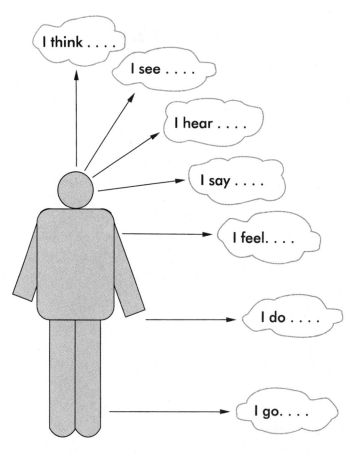

Writing: An Art- and Literature-Based Approach

WRITING

Your Assignment

Tell about someone you know. Put this person in a specific setting (just as Eugenia Collier put Miss Lottie in a flower garden) and situation (just as Eugenia Collier had Miss Lottie being taunted by the children). Write about your person in a way that makes readers understand why you feel as you do about him or her. Vary your sentence beginnings the way Collier does.

Thinking About the Model

Sentence variety adds music to Collier's writing. It also helps make Miss Lottie real. Think about this:

> The most important word in a sentence is the last.
> The second most important word is the first.
> What's in the middle often gets lost.

Thus, sentence beginnings should give important details. Collier's sentences that begin with adjectives add details about Miss Lottie. Those that begin with phrases and clauses describe the setting. Other beginnings zero in on what the children say and do. Collier puts all of this in **logical order.**

Use your character map to help you write the same kinds of sentence beginnings.

Writing Process Tip: Gathering Details

You already know several steps in the writing process. You know that you must first narrow your big topic to a little topic. You know that you must then decide on your purpose and audience. Now, it's time to learn how to **gather details.**

Sometimes finding details means reading newspapers or magazines. Sometimes it means talking to others and asking questions. Sometimes it means brainstorming, pulling ideas from what you already know.

Think about the person you want to write about. Look at your character chart. Which details show most clearly what you want your readers to know? List them in your learning log.

COMPUTER

Some writing programs include characterization word bins. These will help you think of useful details when prewriting and revising.

HINT

Now Write

With your little topic, audience, and purpose in mind, write the first draft of your paper. Use specific details. Include words that tell what you hear, see, smell, taste, and feel.

Get your ideas down. Later, when you revise, you can focus on sentence beginnings.

When you finish your first draft, return to the lesson. You will use Collier's writing as a model to help you revise.

REVISING

Checking Model's Map: Noticing Logical Order

In Chapters 2 and 4, you studied time order and space order. Now look at a third type: logical order.

Logical order comes in two forms. It can show order by **importance** or by **cause and effect.** Collier writes:

> Miss Lottie's marigolds were perhaps the strangest part of the picture. Certainly they did not fit in with the crumbling decay of the rest of her yard.

She has put the most important detail first: marigolds. Less important details about the yard follow. This is an example of one type of logical order—from most important to least important.

Collier also writes:

> Old fears have a way of clinging like cobwebs, and so when we sighted the tumble-down shack, we had to stop to reinforce our nerves.

The logical order here is that of cause and effect. Collier tells why the children had to reinforce their nerves. She explains the cause.

Find details in "Marigolds" that are arranged by importance. Plot them on one of the order-of-importance charts. Then find another example of cause-and-effect order. Map it on a cause-effect chart.

Use the following exercises to help you understand and use logical order.

ORDER-OF-IMPORTANCE MAPS

Most to Least Important:

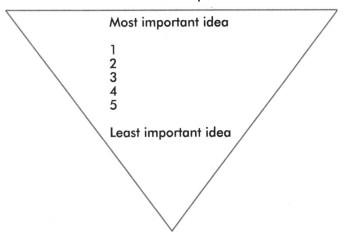

Most important idea

1
2
3
4
5

Least important idea

Least to Most Important

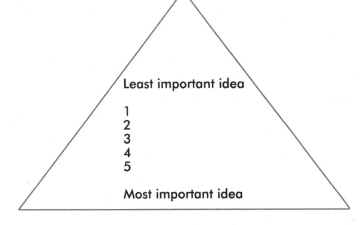

Least important idea

1
2
3
4
5

Most important idea

CAUSE-EFFECT MAP

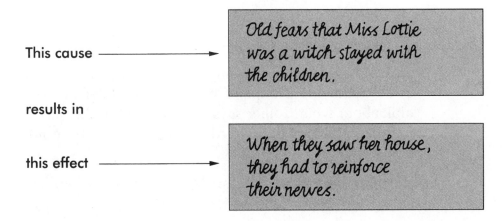

This cause ⟶ Old fears that Miss Lottie was a witch stayed with the children.

results in

this effect ⟶ When they saw her house, they had to reinforce their nerves.

Exercise A—Recognizing Logical Order

Directions. In your learning log, number from 1 to 10. Each of the items below contains sentences that are grouped in logical order. Identify the type of logical order used in each one. Write either "order of importance" or "cause and effect."

1. The children saw Miss Lottie and crept closer to watch. They tossed stones at her and saw her become angry.
2. They noticed first the flowers and then the rest of the garden. Behind it all stood her house.
3. Everything in the garden was well tended, but the marigolds were nearly perfect.
4. She prepared the soil and planted the seed. Later, she watered young plants until they grew and bloomed.
5. Miss Lottie looked like a witch. As children, they thought she was a witch. As they grew older, however, they knew better. Still, she scared them.
6. The narrator was afraid of the old woman. As one of the children who threw stones, she knew it wasn't right. She feels bad about it now.
7. Rows of marigolds grew in the garden. Behind, the house crumbled in decay. A tiny porch stuck out the front of the house. On it sat a rocking chair.
8. The old woman wore a man's hat. She had short white hair like a man's, and she worked like a man.
9. Maybe John Burke was really old. Maybe he was sick. Or maybe he was lazy.
10. As the children enjoyed their youth, they mocked Miss Lottie's age.

Exercise B—Using Logical Order

Directions. In your learning log, number from 1 to 10. Put the following groups of words in the order named. Think about what Collier says. Put yourself in the narrator's place, and put the word groups in order from *her* point of view.

1. (most important to least) Miss Lottie's garden, her marigolds, her house

2. (cause-effect) throwing stones at Miss Lottie, afraid of Miss Lottie, thinking Miss Lottie is a witch

3. (cause-effect) Miss Lottie bent and drawn, tall and powerful, middle aged and full-figured

4. (most important to least) sorry gray house, strip of marigolds, dusty brown yard, sagging roof

5. (least important to most) how she paid for food, how she ate, where food came from, whether she ate

6. (least important to most) weeding, cultivating, arranging

7. (most important to least) John Burke rocked, house crumbled, Miss Lottie weeded, children watched

8. (cause-effects, effects from least to most important) no one visited Miss Lottie, she didn't like intruders, no one talked to her, she didn't take to anyone

9. (effects—in time order—and cause) children whispered about her crazy flowers, children nervous about the witch-woman, made up tales about her, had to annoy her

10. (effects—least important to most—and cause) marigolds interfered with ugliness, they were too beautiful, they said what we didn't understand, they didn't make sense

Exercise C—Applying Logical Order

Directions. In your learning log, number from 1 to 5. Give four details about each of the pictures on pages 72–73. Put the details in one type of logical order: importance or cause-effect. Use each type of order at least once. Name the kind of order you use.

Exercise D—Revising Your Work for Logical Order

Directions. Read your draft. Have you used good order? The order you use will determine how your readers see the person you write about. As you revise, decide if your order meets your purpose. Would another order be better?

Peer-editor Activity. Ask a peer to read your paper for logical order. Can the two of you map the order using one of the logical-order maps above? If not, try to explain why.

Checking the Links: Sentence Beginnings That Show Logical Order

Words and word groups at a sentence beginning can help show logical order. Think about what Eugenia Collier does at the beginning of these sentences to show order:

Certainly they did not fit . . .
Beyond the dusty brown yard . . .
For some perverse reason, we children . . .

Other words and word groups often used at the start of a sentence also show logical order. Some of them are as follows:

more importantly	most importantly
as a result	in the event
consequently	therefore
moreover	at least
in addition	less
least	another
although	still
yet	surely

Certain words followed by nouns (making a phrase) or certain words followed by a subject and verb (making a clause) also show order. Likewise, they add good sentence variety. Here are a few examples:

since + noun = since the beginning, since yesterday (prepositional phrases)

since + noun + verb = since the semester started, since the software came out (adverbial clauses)

because + noun + verb = because the printer was out of toner, because the car had a flat (adverbial clauses)

if + noun + verb = if the truth were known, if everything goes well (adverbial clauses)

The following exercises will let you practice using varied sentence beginnings.

Exercise E—Finding Sentence Beginnings

Directions. In your learning log, number from 1 to 10.

Beside each number write the sentence opener. Then name the type of order it shows. The first one is done for you.

1. Because they were young and didn't know any better, the neighborhood children tormented Miss Lottie.

   Opener: Because they were young and didn't know any better

   Order: cause-effect

2. Even though she was old, Miss Lottie worked faithfully in her garden.

3. Since he was unable to work, John Burke rocked.

4. When the children saw Miss Lottie, they whispered in fear.

5. Although Miss Lottie couldn't hear them from so far away, they still whispered.

6. After the children grew up, they knew they had been cruel to Miss Lottie.

7. Even though they knew of their meanness, they did not apologize.

8. Of course, one can't apologize to a corpse.

9. If Miss Lottie looked a hundred years old when they were children, she wouldn't be alive when they reached adulthood.

10. Did reading about Miss Lottie cause you to think about how you may have treated an older person?

Exercise F—Writing Sentence Beginnings

Directions. In your learning log, number from 1 to 10. Write a good opener for each of the sentences below. Use as many different openers as you can.

1. _____, Miss Lottie probably wasn't as old as the children thought.

2. _____, you may identify with the children.

3. _____, you, too, may wonder why you acted as you did.

4. _____, how do you think Miss Lottie felt?

5. _____, she worked rather hard.

6. _____, John Burke never helped.

As you proofread, remember to check for correct capitalization. In Chapter 1 you learned that proper nouns are capitalized but common nouns are not. Likewise, proper adjectives are capitalized but common adjectives are not. Proper adjectives are formed from proper nouns. For example, notice that Collier refers to Miss Lottie as having *Indian-like features*. *Indian* is a proper adjective and therefore capitalized.

7. _____, the house was in a sad state of decay.

8. _____, probably not many other yards had such pretty flowers.

9. _____, most other gardens had a few vegetables, but no bright colors.

10. _____, the colors made no sense.

Exercise G—Checking Sentence Beginnings in Your Writing

Directions. Compare the sentences in your draft with the sentences in Collier's work. Then compare them with the sentences in the exercises above. Highlight the introductory elements in your sentences (introductory words, phrases, or clauses). Use at least one of each. Revise as needed.

Peer-editor Activity. Ask a peer to read your draft. Ask your editor to suggest at least one more introductory element you can use.

PROOFREADING

Right Reading: Punctuating Introductory Elements

Sentence beginnings, including single words, are often set off with commas. The commas help readers follow the thought.

Study these examples:

> Introductory word:
>> *Yes*, I'll give you a call tonight.
>> *Certainly*, the logic is clear.
>
> Introductory phrase:
>> *During the day*, storm clouds gathered. (prepositional phrase)
>> *Even after trying all morning*, Stephen couldn't get the software to work. (prepositional phrase)
>> *Because of her long hours at work*, Maria carefully organized her time. (prepositional phrase)

Reaching the finish line first, Rick fell from exhaustion. (present participial phrase—i.e., a verb form ending in *-ing* used as an adjective)

Headed for disaster, the driver sped around the curve. (past participial phrase—i.e., a verb form ending in *-ed* used as an adjective)

Introductory clause:

(Remember, a clause must have a subject and a verb.)

When the final curtain fell, the audience burst into applause.

After the emcee introduced the speaker, she sat in the audience.

Because the nights were cool, we wore sweaters to the football game.

If you leave out commas, you can change the meaning. Look at these two examples:

When the final curtain dropped the audience burst into applause.

After the children ate the dog wanted the table scraps.

Now practice punctuating introductory words and word groups.

Exercise H—Commas After Introductory Elements

Directions. In your learning log, number from 1 to 10. Write the introductory element that appears in each of the sentences that follow. Add a comma after each. Then identify the element as a single word, phrase, or clause.

1. Because Miss Lottie worked in her garden the children often saw her bent over.

2. For some reason they thought she looked funny.

3. Even though she was old she managed to bend and stoop, weed and tend.

4. During the long hot summer days the yard grew dusty.

5. Surprisingly the old house looked less drab with the bright marigolds in front of it.

6. For whatever reason the shanty of a house had little care.

7. In spite of the dust and heat Miss Lottie kept the flowers growing and blooming.

8. Obviously she must have watered them.

9. Having said that I wonder how she managed to carry the heavy buckets.

10. Swinging the buckets filled with water she showed her true love for the only real cheer in her life.

Peer-editor Activity. Ask a peer to help you proofread. Check for commas after introductory elements. Check capitalization.

Final Draft

Prepare a final draft, making revisions and proofreading corrections. Use good form. Add a creative title.

Peer/Self-editing Chart

Use the following questions to check your final draft.

1. Did I narrow to a good "little" topic?

2. Have I used specific details, perhaps from my character chart?

3. Did I vary my sentence beginnings?

4. Did I use logical order? Can I identify it?

5. What can I do to make my paper more like Collier's?

Make any final corrections to your work before sharing it with your audience.

SHARING

As a class, put your writing pieces in a book. Decide on a plan for the book. Will you group the works by the subjects' age? By attitude? By location? Choose a logical order.

Write an introduction. Finally, share the book with some of the people about whom you've written.

Portfolio Pointers

Put your final draft in your portfolio. Then, on a separate sheet of paper, answer the following questions.

1. What did I learn about choosing a person to write about?
2. What was hardest about writing this piece?
3. What did I learn about sentence variety?
4. What did a classmate teach me about writing?
5. How can I use what I learned from another writing assignment, either in this class or in another?

Relating Your Writing to the Workplace: Creating a Logical Filing System

Maintaining a sense of order is important in the workplace. A management tool called a flowchart orders details from most important to least important. Budget spreadsheets may show departments alphabetically or by size of budget. Likewise, records must be filed in some order:

alphabetical order:	filed by client or customer name
chronological order:	filed by date of order, date of delivery, or date of payment
numerical order:	filed by invoice number or purchase order number

Choose a local business that interests you. Interview an employee there who keeps some kind of records. Find out in which logical order they are filed. Are the records stored in filing cabinets? On a computer's hard drive? Share your findings with your classmates.

Check the Atlas

Early in "Marigolds," Eugenia Collier writes, "The Depression that gripped the nation was no new thing to us, for the black workers of rural Maryland had always been depressed." Locate Maryland on a United States map. Is Maryland considered part of the North or the

South? Look at the cities and towns named on the map. How much of Maryland do you think is rural today?

Interdisciplinary Interest Project: Raising Marigolds (or Other Annuals)

Miss Lottie knows how to raise great marigolds. What does it take to raise great flowers or vegetables? What do you have to know about plants, preparing the soil, using fertilizer and insecticides, watering, pruning, and weeding?

Choose a plant, such as a tomato, cabbage, petunia, zinnia, or other annual. Check in the library or with a gardening center to find out what is required to raise the plant to maturity so that it blooms and/or bears fruit. If the season is right, or if you have access to a greenhouse, work with a group to try your hand at raising annuals. If not, prepare a report that spells out the process step by step.

chapter 6

Telling

a True Story

PREWRITING

"Of course it's the same old story. Truth usually is the same old story."
Margaret Thatcher, Prime Minister of Great Britain
Time

Visuals

1. "Trampas, New Mexico, Rooms in the House of Juan Lopez, the Mayordomo. Grandfather Romero is 99 Years Old" by John C. Collier, Jr.
2. "On the Subway" by Elizabeth Catlett
3. "The Letter" by Camille Corot
4. "The Lighthouse at Two Lights" by Edward Hopper
5. "Measuring Cup" by Zeke Berman

Your Viewer's Response

Sometimes a picture reminds you of an event in your own life. Choose one of the pictures on pages 92–93, or choose one from a photo album, newspaper, or magazine. What true story does it remind you of? In your learning log, list five or six main points of the true story.

EXAMPLE: someone knocking at door at odd hours

suspect, but no proof

put up motion-sensor lights

neighbors spotted suspect

On the Subway by Elizabeth Catlett

Measuring Cup by Zeke Berman

The Letter by Camille Corot

The Lighthouse at Two Lights by Edward Hopper

Trampas, New Mexico, Rooms in the House of Juan Lopez, the Mayordomo. Grandfather Romero is 99 Years Old by John C. Collier, Jr.

reported to police

knocking stopped

Reading the Literature

A true story can have all of the drama of a fictional story. One way authors build the drama—in both fiction and nonfiction—is to vary their sentence length. Watch for the **sentence variety** as you read.

About the Authors

The Ashabranners have written widely about young people coming to the United States from many different cultures. For the most part, the Ashabranners stay in the background and let people like Tran tell their own stories.

Vocabulary

poled (POHLD) v. moved the boat by pushing into the ocean bottom with a pole

clutched (KLUHCHD) v. held tightly

refugee (ref yoo GEE) n. someone who flees his or her home to find a safer or more pleasant place to live

Excerpt From

THE MOST VULNERABLE PEOPLE

by Brent and Melissa Ashabranner

from *Into a Strange Land: Unaccompanied Refugee Youth in America*

The waves were not big now. Tran sat in the middle of the boat, crowded next to an old woman. She had put her arm around him during the night when the spray from the high waves was cold. He did not know her name. The boat was packed with people standing, sitting, a few lying down, but Tran could see no familiar face. Even now, on their third day at sea, he could not think clearly. He could not really believe what had happened. He knew he was not having a bad dream, but still he hoped he would wake up and be at his home in Vietnam.

The beginning had been good. Late in the afternoon, four days ago, Tran's father had told him they were going fishing, just the two of them. Tran was very happy because he had never been fishing with his father before. Tran's brother, who was ten and four years younger than Tran, cried because his father would not let him come. Tran remembered that his mother stood in the doorway of their house and watched them leave.

An hour later, when it was almost dark, Tran's father led them to a place on the beach where a man was waiting in a small boat. "Hurry," the man said. "You are late."

Tran and his father got into the boat, and the man poled them away from the shore. After awhile, Tran saw a big boat anchored in the bay. They headed toward it, and Tran saw other small boats going in the same direction.

"When are we going to fish?" Tran asked.

"Soon," his father said, "from the big boat."

Tran did not understand, but he said nothing more. Their boat came alongside the big boat; his father and the boatman grabbed a rope ladder from the big boat and pulled their own boat close. Tran's father handed Tran a small plastic bag.

"Climb up the ladder and do not lose the bag," he said.

Tran's eyes widened with fear. "No," he said. "I don't want to."

His father picked him up and swung him to the rope ladder. "I will follow," he said.

Then Tran climbed the ladder, gripping the bag tightly in one hand. When he reached the big boat's rail, two men waiting there swung him onto the deck. Tran saw that the deck was crowded with people. Most were men, but there were also women and children.

Tran looked down and saw that his father was still in the small boat. His father looked up at Tran and raised his hand. "Do not lose the bag," he said.

Then the boatman pushed the small boat away, and soon it was lost in the darkness. Tran cried out to his father, but one of the men standing beside him gripped him roughly by the shoulder. "Do not make noise," he said.

Tran clutched the boat's rail and stared into the night. His heart pounded. Perhaps his father had forgotten something and would return. But in only a few minutes the big boat's engine started up, and the boat moved quickly out to sea. Tran spun away from the rail and tried to run, but people were all around him, and he could hardly move. He held the plastic bag close, and he began to tremble.

It was not until the third day that Tran opened the plastic bag, although it had not been out of his hand, even for a moment. Some of his clothes were in the bag, and there was an envelope. He opened it and found a picture of his family that had been taken last year. He was in the picture with his mother and father, his two sisters, and his brother, Sinh.

A letter from his mother was also in the bag. The letter said she was sorry they could not tell him he was going away. She said the boat would take him to a refugee camp in a place called Thailand. She told him to tell the people who ran the camp that he wanted to go to America. She said she hoped someday the whole family could come or at least his brother when he was older.

Tran held the letter in his hand and stared at it. He knew about refugees. You could not live in Vietnam and not know about them. He had even thought that someday he might be a refugee, but had never imagined that he would leave Vietnam without his family.

Your Reader's Response

Think of a true story that involved you or someone you know. If you could tell Tran the story, what would you say? In your learning log, write three or four sentences that give the main idea of your story.

Springboards for Writing

Use one or both of the following activities to help you write a true story.

Individual Activity. Skim a daily newspaper. Be sure to check at least the headlines in all parts of the paper. Which headlines remind you of a true story you already know? Use a cluster map to keep track of your ideas. In the center, write "Newspaper Stories." In the other bubbles, name stories that the headlines remind you of. If

Writing: An Art- and Literature-Based Approach

you need help, review the cluster maps you have already done.

CLUSTER MAP

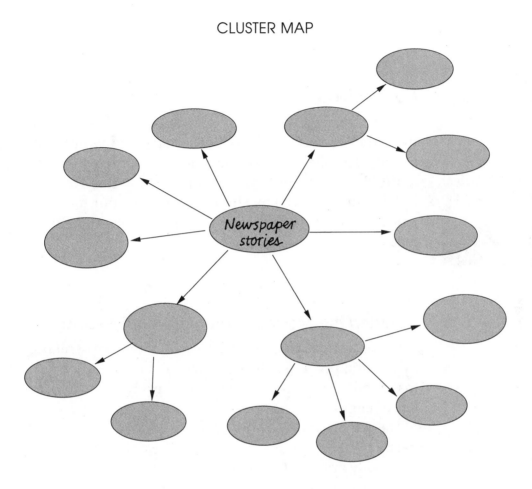

As a class, share your cluster maps. Make notes of any ideas that help you recall a true story. Include your peers' ideas, too.

Group Activity. With two or three peers, divide a piece of paper into four columns. Label the columns the way you would label the parts of a newspaper:

national and international news   sports news
local news   business news

Ask each peer to name a true story that would fit in each column. Be sure the true story is one the peer can tell from his or her own experience. For instance, a foreign exchange student at your school may be the topic for international news. Someone who had an accident makes local news. Someone new on the basketball team makes sports news. The band raising money for a competition tour is business news. Write a headline for each story.

Post the headlines where other class members can review them. Discuss the true-story ideas.

Now Decide

From your Viewer's Response, Reader's Response, or the activities above, pick one true story you would most like to write about. In your learning log, write a topic sentence. Be sure to include the topic and a clue. Like the Ashabranners, you may choose not to put your topic sentence in your story. Writing it now, however, will help you focus on your main idea.

Studying the Model: Sentence Variety—Length

In the last chapter, you learned how to vary sentences by starting them in different ways. It's probably obvious that another way to have **sentence variety** is to vary sentence **length.**

The Ashabranners show important ideas in their writing by putting very short sentences after long ones—or the other way around. Compare these sets of sentences:

> She had put her arm around him during the night when the spray from the high waves was cold. (19 words) He did not know her name. (6 words)

> The beginning had been good. (5 words) Late in the afternoon, four days ago, Tran's father had told him they were going fishing, just the two of them. (21 words)

> An hour later, when it was almost dark, Tran's father led them to a place on the beach where a man was waiting in a small boat. (27 words) "Hurry," the man said. (4 words) "You are late." (3 words)

By putting long sentences next to a short one, the writer gives emphasis to the short one.

Skim the selection. Look for different sentence lengths. Find another pair of sentences like those above. Write the sentences in your learning log and count the words in each. Do the two sentences seem equally important? Does the short sentence seem more important than the long one?

Mapping Your Writing: Plan with a Story Map

A **story map** helps you plan your writing. The following map will help you think about details in the true story you have chosen.

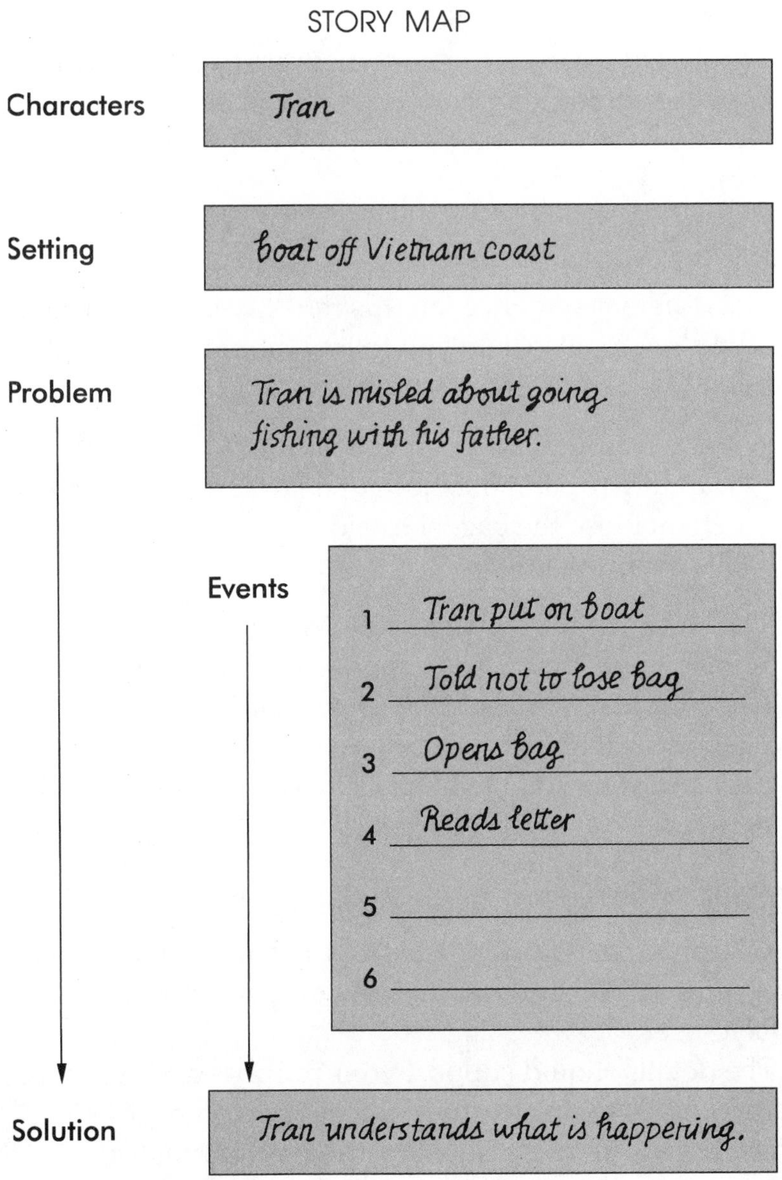

STORY MAP

Characters	Tran

Setting	boat off Vietnam coast

Problem	Tran is misled about going fishing with his father.

Events

1   Tran put on boat
2   Told not to lose bag
3   Opens bag
4   Reads letter
5   _____
6   _____

Solution	Tran understands what is happening.

True stories use names of people, nationalities, and languages. Those names are always capitalized. For instance, <u>T</u>ran, from <u>V</u>ietnam, is on his way to <u>T</u>hailand. There, other <u>V</u>ietnamese refugees wait to go to the <u>U</u>nited <u>S</u>tates. Later they will become <u>A</u>merican citizens. Note the capital letters. Use this as a model for your own writing.

First, list the character(s) and put them in a setting. For instance, Tran, the main character, is on a big boat.

Next, name the problem. For instance, Tran's problem is that he thought he was going fishing with his father but instead has been put on a boat with strangers.

Then name the solution. Tran's problem is resolved when he reads his mother's letter to learn he is a refugee on his way to Thailand.

Finally, list the events that lead to the solution.

WRITING

Your Assignment

Write a true story. It can be something that happened to you or something that happened to someone you know. Build the story's drama varying the length of your sentences.

Thinking About the Model

The different **sentence lengths** the Ashabranners use to tell Tran's story also help you follow the story. Notice that the key ideas are in short sentences:

> The beginning had been good.
> Tran did not understand, but he said nothing more.
> "Do not lose the bag," he said.
> His heart pounded.

The key ideas tell the story **step by step.** You can follow what happened first, what happened next, and what happened after that. The sentence lengths emphasize the step-by-step ideas that help you follow the story.

Use your story map to help you write the same way. Be sure to tell the events step by step.

Writing Process Tip: Choosing Details

Like any other story, a true story has more details than you can put in a short piece. How do you **choose the details** to use?

The details should support your purpose and suit your audience. For example, study the pictures on pages 92–93. Then discuss these questions with your classmates:

Why do you think the artists chose the details pictured? Why do you think the artist of "Trampas, New Mexico" put the man so far back in the picture? How do the details support the artist's purpose? Or in "Measuring Cup," what would happen if the artist had included a folded newspaper in the painting? Would that detail support his purpose?

In your learning log, name the purpose and audience for your true story. Is it to entertain children? To frighten teens? To explain to friends? To make readers think? To show love, appreciation, or concern to relatives?

Make sure every detail you choose fits your purpose and audience.

Now Write

Using your topic sentence and story map, write the first draft of your true story. Follow the story step by step. Use specific details to paint a vivid picture. Use details that support your purpose. Later, when you revise, you can think specifically about sentence length.

When you finish your first draft, return to the lesson. You will use the Ashabranners' writing as a model to help you revise.

REVISING

Checking Model's Map: Following a True Story Step by Step

Readers can follow a true story only if you take them through the events one step at a time. Step-by-step order is a kind of time order. Sometimes, though, the time order only reflects the way in which a person learns about the details—not necessarily the order in which the details happened.

For instance, Tran opens the bag three days after he gets on the boat. As a result, you learn what the letter says days after it was written. Thus, it isn't quite time order, so we call it "step by step."

Use a step-by-step chart to plot what happens in "The Most Vulnerable People."

STEP-BY-STEP CHART

Event 7

Event 6

Event 5

Event 4 *Reads letter*

Event 3 *Opens bag*

Event 2 *Told not to lose bag*

Event 1 *Tran put on board*

As you revise, use the step-by-step chart to map your own writing. Make sure you have put events in a logical order.

Use the following exercise to help to identify and use step by step.

Exercise A—Identifying Step by Step

Directions. In your learning log, number from 1 to 10. Put the following groups of sentences in step-by-step order. You may want to refer to the Ashabranners' story for

Writing: An Art- and Literature-Based Approach

the first six sets. For the rest, you can figure out the step-by-step order on your own. The first set is done for you.

1. *a.* Tran's mother wrote a letter.
   b. Earlier she had taken a family photo.
   c. She enclosed the photo in the letter.
2. *a.* Tran and his father went out in a small boat.
   b. They took the small boat out to a larger boat.
   c. Tran's father promised to take him fishing.
3. *a.* Tran's father promised to follow him up the rope ladder.
   b. Tran didn't want to climb the ladder.
   c. The rope ladder led to the deck of a larger boat.
4. *a.* Tran was scared.
   b. He opened the bag his father had given him.
   c. An old woman tried to comfort him from the wet and cold.
5. *a.* Someone told Tran not to make noise.
   b. He called to his father.
   c. He held on to the rail and watched his father leave.
6. *a.* Three days later he opened the bag.
   b. He found a letter from his mother.
   c. He held on to the bag, not even wondering what was in it.
7. *a.* Tran got seasick.
   b. The boat began to roll.
   c. He vomited until nothing was left in his stomach.
8. *a.* He whispered for water, but no one heard him.
   b. Tran was very thirsty.
   c. The water made him sick again.
9. *a.* Tran didn't eat the rice.
   b. A man gave everyone a cupful of rice.
   c. After he drank the water, he was sick again.
10. *a.* Tran never thought he would leave Vietnam alone.

PUNCTUATION TIP

As you learned in the last chapter, an introductory word group is followed by a comma. Be sure to apply the rule to your own writing as you check for step-by-step words and word groups.

b. He thought someday he would be a refugee.

c. Everyone in Vietnam knew about refugees.

COMPUTER

Many pieces of writing-in-struction software include a sentence-length checker, usually as part of the revision process. Using such software will save you time.

HINT

Checking the Links: Phrases That Show Step by Step

Words and phrases that link step-by-step ideas are similar to the ones that show time order. Notice the ones that the Ashabranners use:

When it was almost dark, Tran's father . . .	(adverbial clause)
Even now . . . he could not think . . .	(introductory words)
After awhile, Tran saw . . .	(prepositional phrase)
Late in the afternoon, . . . Tran's father . . .	(adverb and prepositional phrase)

Sometimes whole sentences show the step-by-step progression:

It was not until the third day that Tran opened . . .

Verbs, too, show step-by-step order. For instance, notice the step-by-step words in this sentence:

He found a picture of his family that *had been taken* (verb) *last year* (adverb).

You'll learn more about verb tense in Chapter 9, but for now remember this:

Verbs show time—present, past, and future. They also show degrees of the past—from the recent past to the distant past. They also show different degrees of the future—from the near future to the distant future.

For example:

Tran *walked* the deck. (past)
Before that, Tran *had walked* on the shore. (more distant past)
Next week Tran *will arrive* in Thailand. (future)
By this time next year, Tran *will have arrived* in the United States. (distant future)

Thus, verbs show time. In that way, they also help show step by step.

The following exercises will help you use step-by-step words.

Exercise B—Identifying Step-by-Step Words

Directions. In your learning log, number from 1 to 10. In the items below, find the words and word groups (phrases and clauses) that show step-by-step order. Write them in your log. You need not list verbs. Note: Some sentences have more than one word or word group that shows step-by-step order.

1. The waves were not big now.
2. She had put her arm around him during the night when the spray from the high waves was cold.
3. Even now, on their third day at sea, he could not think clearly.
4. Late in the afternoon, four days ago, Tran's father had told him they were going fishing.
5. An hour later, when it was almost dark, Tran's father led them to the beach.
6. After awhile, Tran saw a big boat anchored in the bay.
7. Then Tran climbed the ladder.
8. When he reached the boat's rail, two men swung him onto the deck.
9. Then the boatman pushed the small boat away.
10. Soon it was lost in the darkness.

Exercise C—Finding Step-by-Step Verbs

Directions. In your learning log, number from 1 to 10. Beside each number, write the verb or verb phrase from each sentence. Tell whether each is past, distant past, future, or distant future.

1. Waves washed across the deck.
2. Earlier, the ocean spray had drenched Tran.
3. Tran's mother tucked a letter in a bag for him.
4. She had written the letter to give Tran strength.
5. Tran will find a new life in a free country.

6. After leaving Thailand, Tran will travel halfway around the world.
7. By the time Tran becomes a citizen, he will have learned a new language and a new way of life.
8. Tran's family has staked their hope on him.
9. Tran will set the tone for his brother to leave Vietnam.
10. By then, the family will have saved enough money to send their second child to a free land.

Exercise D—Writing Step by Step

Directions. Look at the pictures on pages 92–93. In your learning log, write two sentences about each. Use step-by-step order. The first two are done for you.

1. First we peered through several rooms to where Grandfather Romero sat.
2. Then, as if beckoned by the light from the windows, we tiptoed toward him.

Exercise E—Figuring Sentence Lengths

Directions. Study the following graph for the first two paragraphs in the Ashabranners' work. Then graph the next five paragraphs. What conclusions can you reach about sentence variety?

CHECKING SENTENCE LENGTH

The graph shows the sentence lengths for the first two paragraphs in "The Most Vulnerable People." Note that very long sentences are often followed by very short ones. Why do you think the author does that?

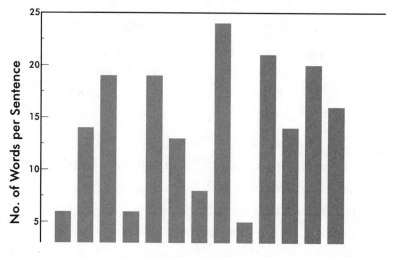

No. of Words per Sentence

Writing: An Art- and Literature-Based Approach

Exercise F—Checking Your Sentence Lengths

Directions. Use the same kind of graph as shown on page 106 to graph your own sentence lengths. Can you revise to make the sentences more varied? Does the length emphasize your ideas? That is, are your most important ideas in the shortest sentences?

Peer-editor Activity. Ask a peer editor to read your draft and look at your graph. Ask him or her to suggest at least one way you can change sentence lengths to emphasize main ideas.

PROOFREADING

Right Reading: Punctuating to Avoid Run-on Sentences

Sometimes new writers trying to vary sentences end up writing run-on sentences. A run-on sentence consists of two sentences stuck together without the right connections. These examples show what is wrong and how to fix it:

Run-on Sentences (wrong):
Tran got seasick on the big ship he couldn't eat.
Tran got seasick on the big ship, he couldn't eat.

Corrected:
Tran got seasick on the big ship. He couldn't eat.
Tran got seasick on the big ship, and he couldn't eat.
Tran got seasick on the big ship; he couldn't eat.

Check out the three ways to fix a run-on sentence:

1. Put in a period and a capital letter. The run-on sentence becomes two complete sentences:
   EXAMPLE: Tran got seasick on the big ship. He couldn't eat.
2. Use a comma and a joining word (called a *coordinating conjunction*) such as *and, but, or, nor, for, yet,* or *so.* You must use **both** the comma and the joining word:
   EXAMPLE: Tran got seasick on the big ship, and he couldn't eat.

COMPUTER

If you have writing-program software that counts or graphs words per sentence, use it for your own writing. Put the count or graph in your portfolio. Later you can compare another piece of writing with this one. Check for improvement.

HINT

3. Use a semicolon to separate the two parts of the run-on sentence. The two parts must be closely related to use the semicolon. The second part should be a result of the first:

> EXAMPLE: Tran got seasick on the big ship, he couldn't eat.

Use the following exercises to practice finding and correcting run-on sentences.

Exercise G—Finding Run-on Sentences

Directions. In your learning log, number from 1 to 10. If a group of words makes a run-on sentence, write "run-on" in your log. If not, write "okay."

1. Tran's father hurried toward the beach with Tran they met a boatman who took them both aboard.
2. When they reached the big boat, Tran climbed up the rope ladder to the deck.
3. Tran called out to his father, someone on deck told him to be quiet.
4. He huddled on deck next to a woman who put her arms around him to keep him warm then he finally fell asleep.
5. The rough water made the ship toss and roll and Tran became so seasick that he could neither eat nor drink.
6. Three days passed on the crowded deck Tran finally opened the bag to see what it held.
7. When he opened the bag, he found clothes and a letter from his mother.
8. The clothes were all he had with him from home he wondered how he would manage.
9. The letter said he should go to the United States but first he would go to Thailand.
10. Tran always thought his family would leave Vietnam together, never did he think he would go alone.

Exercise H—Correcting Run-on Sentences

Directions. Reread the sentences above that you marked as run-on sentences. In your learning log, rewrite them to correct the error.

Exercise I—Checking Your Writing for Run-on Sentences

Directions. Read your paper carefully. Watch for run-on sentences. Correct any that you find.

Peer-editor Activity. Ask a peer to read your paper for any run-on sentences you might have missed. Correct any that he or she finds.

Final Draft

Prepare a final draft, making revisions and proofreading corrections. Use good form. Add a catchy title.

Peer/Self-editing Chart

Use the following questions to check your final draft.

1. Have I used specific details to paint a clear picture for my reader?
2. Did I tell a good story with events that lead to a solution to the character's problem?
3. Are the events in step-by-step order?
4. Have I used a variety of sentence lengths?
5. Have I avoided run-on sentences?
6. Can I do anything to make my story more like the Ashabranners'?

Make any final corrections to your true story before sharing it with your audience.

SHARING

As a class, put your true stories into newspaper form. Group the stories into front-page news, sports news, business news, and so on. Write headlines for each. Humorous true stories can be turned into cartoons. Share your newspaper with the media center.

Portfolio Pointers

Put your final draft into your portfolio. On a separate sheet of paper, answer the following questions:

1. What did I learn about telling a true story?
2. As I wrote this story, what was hardest for me?

If you have a CD-ROM reference library—especially one that includes an encyclopedia, cultural literacy dictionary, or biographical dictionary—try keyword searches to find information about historical periods, refugee groups, or immigrants. Use cross references to find additional information.

HINT

3. What did I learn about sentence length?

4. What did a classmate teach me about writing?

Relating Your Writing to the Workplace: Giving Directions

Printed directions tell you how to program your new VCR. The owner's manual tells you how to care for your car. Instructions tell you how to build a model airplane.

The person who wrote these directions, manuals, and instructions is called a technical writer. Find a manual, a set of directions, or instructions. With a peer, read it carefully. Discuss what you found with the class. Do you think you could be a technical writer? Explain.

Try your hand at planning a piece of technical writing.

HOW TO . . .

Project   *Record Message on Telephone Answering Machine*

Materials Needed	Steps	Results
1 *Answering machine*	1 *Plan message*	*Message to callers*
2 *Blank audio tape*	2 *Connect power and telephone to answering machine*	
3	3 *Insert audio tape*	
4	4 *Press "Record"*	
5	5 *Read message*	
6	6 *Test by pressing "Record" and "Play"*	

Check the Atlas

On a world map, locate Vietnam. Find Thailand. Then find the closest route to the United States. If Tran went from his homeland in Vietnam to the nearest point in the U.S., how far would he have traveled? What bodies of water would he have crossed?

Interdisciplinary Interest Project: Boat People and Other Refugees

Tran stands for thousands of young people whose families bought them passage to the United States. Because they left Vietnam in the dark of night, fleeing for their lives on almost any vessel that floated, they came to be called "boat people." Over many decades, other refugees have fled to the United States from other countries. Many of us are descendants of those refugees.

Choose a period in history and an ethnic group of refugees which interests you. Research their background. Why did they leave their native country? How did they reach the United States? What happened after they arrived? If possible, talk to someone who was a refugee or whose parents were refugees. Ask that person to tell you his or her story. Perhaps he or she will tell it to the class.

Use the KWL chart to help you plan.

KWL CHART

Subject		
K What I Know	W What I Want to Know	L What I Learned

chapter 7

Sharing

a Learning Experience

PREWRITING

Visuals

1. "Woman Playing with a Cat" by Kaigetsudo Dohan
2. "Untitled (Pole Vaulter)" by Alexander Rodchenko
3. "Untitled" by Steve Catron
4. "Thanksgiving" by Doris Lee
5. "Study for Aspects of Negro Life: The Negro in an African Setting" by Aaron Douglas

"There are three ingredients in the good life: learning, earning, and yearning."

Christopher Morley, novelist

Your Viewer's Response

Choose one of the pictures. Or choose one of your own from a photo album, book, or magazine. Let the picture remind you of something you have experienced. What did you learn as a result? In your learning log, write two sentences. In the first, explain what happened. In the second, tell what you learned.

EXAMPLE: During a tornado, our family took cover in the basement.

I learned that we could be safe even

Study for Aspects of Negro Life: The Negro in an African Setting by Aaron Douglas

Thanksgiving by Doris Lee

Untitled by Steve Catron

Woman Playing with a Cat by
Kaigetsudo Dohan

Untitled (Pole Vaulter) by
Alexander Rodchenko

SPELLING TIP

The letter *c* can sound like *s* or like *k*.

In general the letter *c* . . .

—followed by a consonant or the vowels *a*, *o*, or *u* sounds like *k*: *cat, cot, cut* or *climb, crash.*

—followed by *e*, *i*, or *y* sounds like *s*: *cent, civil, cycle.*

—followed by *h* sounds like *ch* as in *chin* or *k* as in *chord.*

though the house was partly blown away.

Reading the Literature

In this passage, Rudolfo Anaya shares a learning experience. As you read, watch how he uses two subjects, two objects, two adjectives, or two sentences. The **compound parts** give a good rhythm to the writing, making it almost musical.

About the Author

Telling about his Latin American culture is a passion for Rudolfo A. Anaya (1937–). Much of his writing is set in New Mexico, so it gives a clear blend of the old and new Southwest.

Vocabulary

llano (LAH no) n. large, level, grassy plain

Panhandle (PAN han duhl) n. the part of Oklahoma shaped like the handle of a pan

arroyos (uh ROY ohs) n. dry gullies or streams

juniper and **piñon trees** (JOO ni per, PEEN yahn) n. evergreen trees common in the Southwest

vast (VAST) adj. quite large

cicadas (si KAY duhz) n. large insects that in the summer make a shrill buzzing sound

herbs (ERBS) n. plants used for medicine or seasoning

intoned (in TOHND) v. chanted, spoke in a singing tone

curandera (koo rahn DE ruh) n. Hispanic healer who uses folk medicine to treat patients

BACKGROUND CONVERSATION NOTES

By Rudolfo Anaya

from *Writing the Southwest*

edited by David King Dunaway and
Sara L. Spurgeon

The llano is not exactly flat. It's not the plains country of the Panhandle or of Kansas. It's more rolling hills, arroyos, juniper and piñon trees. It has that spectacular beauty that any stage has. I view the llano as a stage that is empty. It seemed to me as a child I would look out across the llano and I would see nothing, and then people would enter. Somebody would come driving down the dirt road in a pickup truck to visit my father, and my father would come from the house, and soon there was a dramatic happening on that vast and empty land.

The sound of the llano is silence. It's a silence created by a buzz, and the buzz to me is the sound of the earth. If you stand very still, as I did when I was a child, I could actually feel the earth turning. Then I had to think, What is this sound, and what is it telling me? And then of course, if you listen very closely, the sound becomes the sound of grasshoppers, of cicadas, the wind rustling across the grass, the tinkling of a bell on a goat, lizards darting here and there, and suddenly you realize that that silence, that sound, is the sound of life itself.

COMPUTER

As you study the vocabulary, use your on-line thesaurus to find other synonyms and antonyms to help you understand the definitions.

HINT

Excerpt From

BLESS ME, ULTIMA
by Rudolfo Anaya

Ultima came to stay with us the summer I was almost seven. When she came the beauty of the llano unfolded before my eyes, and the gurgling waters of the river sang to the hum of the turning earth. The magical time of childhood stood still, and the pulse of the living earth pressed its mystery into my living blood. She took my hand, and the silent, magic powers she possessed made beauty from the raw, sun-baked llano, the green river valley, and the blue bowl which was the white sun's home. . . .

There is a time in the last few days of summer when the ripeness of autumn fills the air, and time is quiet and mellow. I lived that time fully, strangely aware of a new world opening up and taking shape for me. In the mornings, before it was too hot, Ultima and I walked in the hills of the llano, gathering the wild herbs and roots for her medicines. We roamed the entire countryside and up and down the river. . . .

For Ultima, even the plants had a spirit, and before I dug she made me speak to the plant and tell it why we pulled it from its home in the earth. "You that grow well here in the arroyo by the dampness of the river, we lift you to make good medicine," Ultima intoned softly and I found myself repeating after her. . . .

Ultima's soft hands would carefully lift the plant and examine it. She would take a pinch and taste its quality. . . . She told me that the dry contents of her bag contained a pinch of every plant she had ever gathered since she began her training as a curandera many years ago.

Your Reader's Response

The narrator learns much from Ultima. Think of someone from whom you've learned. What did you learn? Respond in your learning log.

Springboards for Writing

Use the following to help you remember a good learning experience.

Individual Activity. Aristotle said, "What we have to learn to do, we learn by doing." Look in a dictionary of quotations to see what others have said about learning. Use their statements to help you remember a learning experience of your own.

For instance, the Aristotle quotation might describe the way you learned to use word processing software. Instead of reading the manual, maybe you learned at the keyboard. You clicked on each menu until you discovered the right command to do what you wanted. You learned by *doing*.

In your learning log, write the quotation and source. In three to five sentences, describe the learning experience it reminds you of.

Share your quotations with the class.

Group Activity. In a small group, share your learning

Internet Connection

You can find other books of quotations at On-line Reference Works at http://www.cs.cmu.edu/Web/references.html.

The address for Bartlett's Familiar Quotations is http://www.columbia.edu/acis/bartleby/bartlett/.

CLUSTER MAP

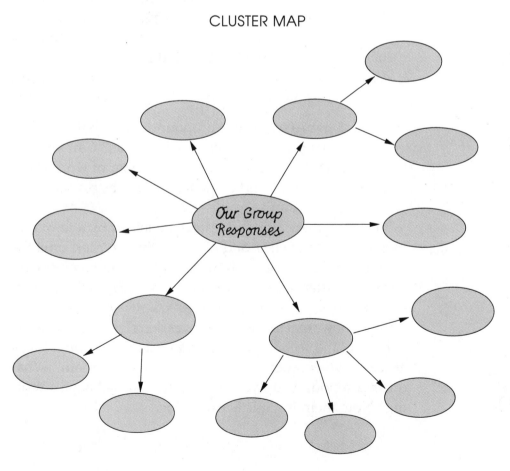

Our Group Responses

When two or more adjectives describe the same noun, they are called *coordinate adjectives*. Use a comma between coordinate adjectives.

To test for coordinate adjectives, insert the word *and* between the adjectives. If it sounds okay, the words are coordinate. And if the words can be reversed, they are coordinate.

EXAMPLES:

1. A deep wide channel cut through the islands.

To check: The channel is deep and wide. The channel is wide and deep. (coordinate adjectives; use a comma)

2. A red race car sped past.

To check: The car is red and race. (not coordinate adjectives; use no comma)

---

log response to the visuals or to the literary selection. As each peer shares a log entry, others should tell what learning experience it triggered for them. Keep track of the responses on a cluster map.

Now Decide

From your Viewer's Response, Reader's Response, or the activities above, pick one learning experience you would most like to write about. In your learning log, write two sentences. The first should identify the experience. The second should tell what you learned.

Studying the Model: Compound Parts

Rudolfo Anaya connects many ideas by using **compound parts.** He will put two words, two groups of words, or even two sentences together to make compounds. The effect is pleasing to the mind and to the ear. For instance, in the first paragraph, Anaya writes the following:

It is not the plains country *of the Panhandle* or *of Kansas.*
(two prepositional phrases)
It's more rolling hills, *arroyos, juniper* and *piñon trees.*
(four nouns)
I would look out across the llano and *I would see nothing.* . . .　　　　　　　(two sentences)
. . . that *vast* and *empty* land . . .　　(two adjectives)

Notice how Anaya puts compound parts together. Can you hear how the parts sound nearly alike? Can you see how the parts have about the same number of words? For instance, the compound sentences above begin the same way: *I would look* and *I would see.*

Note, too, that compound parts are joined by a few common words: *and, but, or,* and *nor.* Sometimes writers omit the joining word and use a comma to separate short compound parts. For instance, Anaya refers to "the *silent, magic* powers she possessed." You know he means *silent and magic.* But the comma shows that the two adjectives describe the same noun.

Look at the second paragraph in Anaya's writing. It has at least five compound parts. Can you find them? What other compounds do you find in the rest of Anaya's writing? Note them in your learning log.

Mapping Your Writing: Plan with a Learning-experience Map

Use the learning-experience map to help you think through your own learning experience. Like a good newspaper reporter, you must tell your readers the key points: who, what, where, when, and why. The "why" is what you learned.

LEARNING-EXPERIENCE MAP

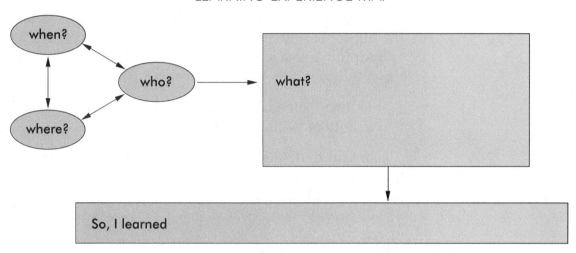

WRITING

Your Assignment

Share a learning experience. Like Rudolfo Anaya, set the background. Explain what happened. In other words, tell who, what, when, and where. Then show what you learned—the "why."

Maybe you learned how to be happy or make others happy even when the world seems gloomy. Maybe you learned how to resolve a conflict, or how to cope with some everyday problem. Perhaps you discovered what is really important to you or to others around you.

Like Anaya, use compound parts to help explain what you learned.

Thinking About the Model

The **compound parts** that Anaya uses make good reading. The pairs of words, word groups, and sentences put **similar ideas** together. That gives writing a rhythm, like music.

Try putting the same kind of music in your writing.

Writing Process Tip: Developing Big-topic Sentences

In Chapter 1 you learned about topic sentences. You learned that each has a subject and a clue. Each paragraph has a topic sentence.

There is also a larger kind of topic sentence. If you are writing a longer piece—with more than one paragraph—you need a kind of topic sentence for the whole piece. It is properly called a *thesis sentence,* but you can think of it as the **big-topic sentence.**

Rudolfo Anaya's big-topic sentence is something like this:

> Ultima helped me understand even more of the beauty of the llano than I already knew.

Can you find Anaya's little topic sentences for each of his paragraphs in *Bless Me, Ultima?*

TOPIC-SENTENCE MAP

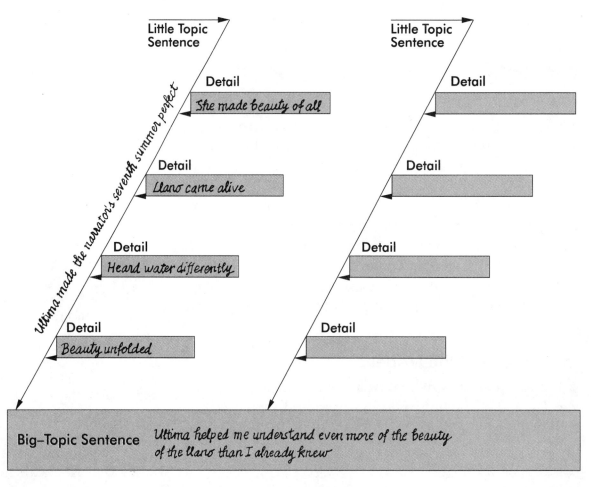

Writing: An Art- and Literature-Based Approach

Make your own topic-sentence map. Write your big-topic sentence across the bottom. Then add the little-topic sentences.

Now Write

Using the topic-sentence map as your guide, write the first draft of your learning experience. Use compound parts to show similar ideas. Make sure that the details explain the topic sentences and fit your purpose and audience.

When you finish the first draft, return to the lesson. You will use Anaya's writing as a model to help you revise.

REVISING

Checking Model's Map: Compounds to Show Similarity

Some compounds show how ideas are alike. They are usually joined with the word *and*. Other compounds show how ideas are different. They are usually joined with the word *but*. Still other compounds show choices. They are usually joined with the words *or* or *nor*.

Rudolfo Anaya uses all three compounds, but he uses them mostly to show similarity.

Use the map below to trace Anaya's words, word groups, and sentences that show ideas that are alike.

PUNCTUATION TIP

Remember, when you put two sentences together with a joining word such as *and*, *but*, *or*, or *nor*, you must use a comma. Follow Anaya's example.

> . . . I would see nothing, and then people would enter.

If you join two predicates, however, do **not** use a comma. (A predicate is the verb, its objects, and any modifiers.) For example, in another passage, Anaya writes the following:

> I defined my cultural identity for myself and knew it within myself. . . .

The two predicates *defined my cultural identity for myself* and *knew it within myself* have no comma between them.

COMPOUNDS TO SHOW SIMILARITIES

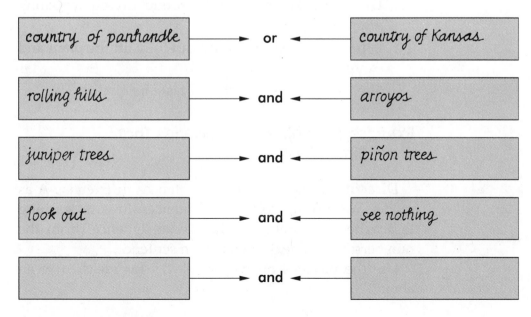

Use the following exercises to practice what you have learned about compound parts.

Exercise A—Recognizing Compound Parts

Directions. In your learning log, number from 1 to 15. Write the compound parts in each of these sentences.

1. Ultima came to stay with us for the summer and to teach me her love of the land.
2. The beauty of the llano unfolded before my eyes, and the gurgling waters of the river sang to the hum of the earth.
3. Ripeness of autumn fills the air, and time lingers long.
4. Time is quiet and mellow.
5. A new world was opening up and taking shape for me.
6. I lived that time fully, strangely aware.
7. Ultima and I walked in the hills of the llano.
8. We gathered the wild herbs and roots for her medicines.
9. We roamed the entire countryside and along the river.
10. We roamed up and down the river.
11. For Ultima, even the plants had a spirit; and before I dug, she made me speak to the plant.
12. She made me speak to the plant and tell it why we pulled it from its home in the earth.
13. Ultima spoke softly, and I found myself repeating after her.
14. Ultima's soft hands would carefully lift the plant and examine it.
15. She would take a pinch and taste its quality.

Exercise B—Writing Compounds That Show Similarities

Directions. Use five of the sentences in Exercise A as models for writing your own sentences. In your learning log, write the number of the model sentence (from the numbers above) next to your own sentence.

Use the pictures on pages 114–115 for ideas to write about.

Checking the Links: Words and Word Groups That Show Similarities (and Differences)

You already know that of the four common joining words, one shows similarities (*and*) and three show differences (*but, or,* and *nor*).

Other words and word groups also show similarities and differences. Some of the common ones are listed here:

Similarities	Differences
besides	however
also	on the one hand
what's more	on the other hand
furthermore	nevertheless
in addition	rather
again	on the contrary
for example	yet
in other words	by contrast
in the same way	except for
similarly	not
likewise	

The following exercises let you practice finding and using good links.

Exercise C—Identifying Linking Words

Directions. In your learning log, number from 1 to 10. Identify the linking word or words in the following sentences by writing them in your log. Hint: Some sentences have more than one.

1. Ultima taught the narrator to love the earth's plants in the same way she did.
2. The narrator describes the llano as comfortable, in other words, as home.
3. If the sound of the llano is silence and if the silence is the buzz of the earth, he can hear the earth turn.
4. If he can hear the earth turn, then can he also hear the sunrise and sunset?
5. Lizards dart here and there, yet they are part of the silence.

6. The silence becomes the sound of grasshoppers and cicadas in the same way that the silence becomes the wind rustling across the grass or the tinkling of a bell on a goat.

7. The silence is the sound of life itself, not necessarily, however, the sound of human life.

8. Anaya wondered what the sound of silence was telling him, and Ultima put a voice to it.

9. On the one hand the magical time of childhood stood still, but on the other hand the living earth pressed its mystery into the narrator's living blood.

10. There is a time in the last few days of summer when the ripeness of autumn fills the air, and time is quiet and mellow.

Exercise D—Identifying Similarity or Difference

Directions. Return to your learning log and look at the answers you wrote for Exercise C. Beside each, tell whether the link shows similarity or difference.

Exercise E—Checking Compound Parts in Your Writing

Directions. Earlier, you made a map to show which of Anaya's compounds showed similarities. Complete a similar map of your own compounds, showing the similarities and differences. On the map, show your compound words, word groups, and sentences. Show your joining words, too.

Peer-editor Activity. Ask a peer to read your paper and study your compound map. Then ask him or her to suggest at least two more places where you can add similar ideas and form a compound part. Revise as needed.

PROOFREADING

Right Reading: Punctuating a Compound or a Series

Review the punctuation tips above. The first tells you about commas with coordinate adjectives. Anaya writes of the "raw, sun-baked llano." *Raw* and *sun-baked* both describe the llano.

The second punctuation tip reminds you to use a comma with a joining word when you write compound sentences. (See Chapter 6, Proofreading, to review how to avoid run-on sentences.)

Sometimes, however, compounds have three or more parts. Then they form a series. Use commas between items in a series, as Anaya does:

> The llano is more rolling hills, arroyos, juniper and piñon trees.

The commas separate items in the series. Observe that there is no comma after *juniper.* Anaya uses journalistic style. Other writers may put a comma there. You will be right either way.

Sometimes the series is complicated. Study Anaya's sentence here:

> The sound becomes the sound
> > of grasshoppers,
> > of cicadas,
> > the wind rustling across the grass,
> > the tinkling of a bell on a goat,
> > lizards darting here and there,
> and suddenly you realize that that silence, that
> sound, is the sound of life itself.

In this case, Anaya has five items in the series. The series is followed by a comma and a joining word after *there* to begin another compound part—a compound sentence!

These sentences identify a sophisticated writer.

Use the following exercise to practice punctuating a compound or a series.

Exercise F—Adding Punctuation to a Compound or Series

Directions. In your learning log, number from 1 to 10. Copy the following sentences and add commas where needed. Hint: Many sentences need more than one comma, and some sentences need no commas.

1. When I was seven, Ultima came for the summer and she taught me that the plants had a spirit.
2. During that summer, Ultima showed me how to harvest plants and preserve them for later use.
3. We harvested plants in the early morning in the late evening and on cloudy days.
4. Ultima had silent magic powers and taught them to me.
5. She made everything beautiful and I learned to see the llano the river valley and the sky through her eyes.
6. Before it was too hot, we walked the hills gathering wild herbs roots and leaves for her medicines.
7. Ultima spoke to the plants told them why she was digging them and stored a pinch of each in her bag.
8. Do you think Anaya writes about personal cultural topics or does he write just to entertain?
9. Do you think you would like to spend a summer walking with Ultima working alongside her and learning from her?
10. Do you think you would like the silent mysterious land of the llano?

Peer-editor Activity. Ask a peer editor to check your work for commas with coordinate adjectives, series, and compound sentences. Revise as needed.

Final Draft

Prepare a final draft, making revisions and proofreading corrections. Use good form. Add a creative title.

Peer/Self-editing Chart

Use the following questions to check your final draft.

1. Did I use a good big-topic sentence?
2. Did I use a good topic sentence for each paragraph?
3. Did I use specific details to explain my topic sentences?
4. Did I use compound parts to show similar ideas?
5. Did I use good linking words to show similar or different ideas?
6. Did I use commas whenever I used a coordinate adjective, series, or compound sentence?
7. What can I do to make my writing more like Anaya's?

Make final corrections to your learning experience before sharing it with your audience.

SHARING

Learning experiences are fun to share. Read your finished paper to an older relative or friend, preferably a senior citizen. Ask that person, in turn, to share one of his or her own learning experiences with you. Then, with your peers, share the stories you heard.

For added interest, you may want to turn the stories into a collection of memorable quotes, like *Bartlett's Familiar Quotations.*

Portfolio Pointers

Put your final draft into your portfolio. Then, on a separate sheet of paper, answer the following questions:

1. What strengths does this piece show about my writing?
2. What was the biggest problem for me in writing this piece? How did I solve it?
3. What did this piece teach me about writing?
4. How can I use what I learned in other areas of my school work?

Relating Your Writing to the Workplace: Daily Work Logs

Daily work logs are part of many jobs. In a way, they help employees and employers learn from their experiences. For instance, a nurse's work log may record a patient's blood pressure, temperature, and heart rate. It may also include notes about what the nurse saw (such as, "Patient slept poorly, ate only a few bites at lunch," and so on). On the other hand, a refrigerator technician's work log may record date, time, and address of service calls. It may also include a list of repairs made, parts used, and billing invoice numbers for each call.

Talk to friends and relatives about their jobs. What other jobs require a daily work log? Share your findings with the class. If possible, bring to class a sample log or a photocopy of a completed log.

Check the Atlas

On a map of the United States, locate New Mexico. What other states make up the Southwest? What major cities do you find in New Mexico? What kind of terrain does the map show? Desert? Mountains? Canyons? If you live outside New Mexico, what does the map tell you about New Mexico that is different from where you live?

Interdisciplinary Interest Project: Plants and Herbal Remedies

Rudolfo Anaya writes about the herbs that Ultima uproots. Many cultures have used herbal medicines to treat various hurts and ailments. Alternative medicine, which includes some herbal remedies, brings relief to some. More significantly, scientists remind us that the rain forests may hold the secrets to curing such diseases as cancer.

Interview someone who is familiar with the use of plants and herbs as health aids. Or check the library for information. Then choose one herbal remedy that interests you. Share the information with your classmates. Be able to name the herb, tell where you can find it, and explain how it can be used as a health aid. Compile a class list.

Writing: An Art- and Literature-Based Approach

chapter 8

Writing

a Conversation

PREWRITING

> **Visuals**
>
> 1. "Three Quilters (Quilting Party)" by John Biggers
> 2. "Nighthawks" by Edward Hopper
> 3. "Table for Four" by Daniel Franks
> 4. "Saguaros, Saguaro National Monument" by Ansel Adams
> 5. "The Nut Gatherers" by Adolphe William Bouguereau

> *"I just use my muscles as a conversation piece, like someone walking a cheetah down 42nd Street."*
> Arnold Schwarzenegger, body builder
> *News Summary*

Your Viewer's Response

Choose one of the pictures. Imagine that a person—or object—is talking. Give him or her a name. Imagine that he or she is talking to someone.

In your learning log, fold a page in half lengthwise. Label the first column by the person's (or object's) name. Label the second column with the name of the person spoken to. In the first column, write the words you think the person or object might say. In the second column, write the response.

Nighthawks by Edward Hopper

Table for Four
by Daniel Franks

Saguaros, Saguaro National Monument by
Ansel Adams

Three Quilters (Quilting Party)
by John Biggers

The Nut Gatherers
by Adolphe-William
Bouguereau

EXAMPLE:

Bob Cactus	Claude Cactus
Hey, Claude! Some heat, huh?	Right you are! I think my needles are wilting.
Maybe you need some mousse to keep 'em all in place.	Actually a good rain would help as much as anything.

Reading the Literature

Good conversation makes good storytelling. As you read this selection, watch the **paragraphing in dialogue.** It helps you keep track of who is talking.

About the Author

Journalist, civil rights worker, and author, Maya Angelou (1928–) has written five autobiographical books. In the most popular of them, *I Know Why the Caged Bird Sings*, she writes about her experiences growing up as an African American in Arkansas.

Vocabulary

provisions (proh VIZH uhns) n. stock of food

clarity (KLAR uh tee) n. clearness

infuse (in FYOOZ) v. to put ideas into; to fill with meaning

valid (VAL id) adj. sound, logical

boggled (BAHG uhld) v. startled or frightened

abuse (uh BYOOZ) v. mistreat

outhouse (OUT hows) n. a small building used for toilet purposes when the nearby house has no plumbing

leered (LIRD) v. stared

Internet Connection

You may want to consider other pieces of art for this activity. You can find dozens of options if you go to the following URL: http://www.yahoo.com/Arts/Art-History/Artists/ Choose from among painters, photographers, sculptors, and illustrators.

Excerpt From

I KNOW WHY THE CAGED BIRD SINGS

by Maya Angelou

One summer afternoon, sweet-milk fresh in my memory, [Mrs. Flowers] stopped at the Store to buy provisions. Another Negro woman of her health and age would have been expected to carry the paper sacks home in one hand, but Momma said, "Sister Flowers, I'll send Bailey up to your house with these things."

She smiled that slow dragging smile, "Thank you, Mrs. Henderson. I'd prefer Marguerite, though." My name was beautiful when she said it. "I've been meaning to talk to her, anyway." They gave each other age-group looks.

Momma said, "Well, that's all right then. Sister, go and change your dress. You going to Sister Flowers'. . . ."

There was a little path beside the rocky road, and Mrs. Flowers walked in front swinging her arms and picking her way over the stones.

She said, without turning her head, to me, "I hear you're doing very good school work, Marguerite, but that it's all written. The teachers report that they have trouble getting you to talk in class." We passed the triangular farm on our left and the path widened to allow us to walk together. I hung back in the separate unasked and unanswerable questions.

"Come and walk along with me, Marguerite." I couldn't have refused even if I wanted to. She pronounced my name so nicely. Or more correctly, she spoke each word with such clarity that I was certain a foreigner who didn't understand English could have understood her.

"Now no one is going to make you talk—possibly no one can. But bear in mind, language is man's way of communicating with his fellow man and it is language alone which separates him from the lower animals." That was a totally new idea to me, and I would need time to think about it.

"Your grandmother says you read a lot. Every chance you get. That's good, but not good enough. Words mean more than what is set down on paper. It takes the human voice to infuse them with the shades of deeper meaning."

I memorized the part about the human voice infusing words. It seemed so valid and poetic.

She said she was going to give me some books and that I not only must read them, I must read them aloud. She suggested that I try to make a sentence sound in as many different ways as possible.

"I'll accept no excuse if you return a book to me that has been badly handled." My imagination boggled at the punishment I would deserve if in fact I did abuse a book of Mrs. Flowers'. Death would be too kind and brief.

The odors in the house surprised me. Somehow I had never connected Mrs. Flowers with food or eating or any other common experience of common people. There must have been an outhouse, too, but my mind never recorded it.

The sweet scent of vanilla had met us as she opened the door.

"I made tea cookies this morning. You see, I had planned to invite you for cookies and lemonade so we could have this little chat. The lemonade is in the icebox."

It followed that Mrs. Flowers would have ice on an ordinary day, when most families in our town bought ice late on Saturdays only a few times during the summer to be used in the wooden ice-cream freezers.

She took the bags from me and disappeared through the kitchen door. I looked around the room that I had never in my wildest fantasies imagined I would see. Browned photographs leered or threatened from the walls and the white, freshly done curtains pushed against themselves and against the wind. I wanted to gobble up the room entire and take it to Bailey, who would help me analyze and enjoy it.

"Have a seat, Marguerite. Over there by the table." She carried a platter covered with a tea towel. Although she warned that she hadn't tried her hand at baking sweets for some time, I was certain that like everything else about her the cookies would be perfect.

Your Reader's Response

You learn about people from what they say and do. For instance, Mrs. Flowers' words and actions show that she cares about Marguerite. If you could talk with someone like Mrs. Flowers, whom would it be?

In your learning log, fold a page in half lengthwise. Put your name at the top of the left column. Put the name of someone like Mrs. Flowers at the top of the right column. Write an imaginary conversation between the two of you. Use the example in Your Viewer's Response as a model.

Springboards for Writing

One or both of the following activities will help you write a good conversation.

Individual Activity. Read the comic page in a daily newspaper. Or review a comic book. Study the conversation. Next, choose two characters of your own—real or imaginary. (If you wish, you may use the characters from the Reader's Response.)

In your learning log, draw a cartoon strip with at least five frames. You can use stick figures or just faces. To show which character is which, you can do something as simple as putting a hat on one. Add dialogue bubbles.

Group Activity. Choose a picture from pages 132–133 or another that has two to four characters in it. With one to four peers, take the roles of the characters pictured. Here's how:

Divide a sheet of paper into columns. Make as many columns as there are characters. Give each character a name. Put the name at the top of the column. Each of you will take the role of a character. Draw straws to decide the order in which you will "talk."

Then, without talking aloud, pass the paper from peer to peer. Write your dialogue in the appropriate columns.

When you finish, share your conversation with the class. Each of you should read your respective role part. Be sure to identify the picture you chose.

Now Decide

From your Viewer's Response, Reader's Response, or the activities above, pick two people (real or imaginary) who can talk to one another. In your learning log, write two sentences. In the first, tell who the characters will be. In the second, say what they will talk about.

Studying the Model: Paragraphs in Dialogue

As you read Maya Angelou's dialogue, you may have noticed that her paragraphs are short. They seem to have

COMPUTER

If possible, e-mail your lines of dialogue to one another. Instead of columns, change fonts to show who is talking. When you finish, print a copy. Share aloud with the class.

HINT

no topic sentence. That's because **paragraphs in dialogue** break with each change of speaker.

Review the first three paragraphs of Angelou's work. Note that the first paragraph has words by Momma. In the second, it is Mrs. Flowers talking. In the third, it is Momma again.

The rest of the selection is all dialogue spoken by Mrs. Flowers. Marguerite never speaks. But you do read her thoughts.

Why do you think Angelou breaks the paragraphs as she does? With two or three peers, talk about possible reasons. Share your reasons with the rest of the class.

Mapping Your Writing: Plan with a Dialogue Flowchart

Use the dialogue flowchart to plan your conversation. Be sure to put in the names of Character One and Character Two.

DIALOGUE FLOWCHART

Character 1:

name: _Bob Cactus_

Character 2:

name: _Claude Cactus_

Hey, Claude! Some heat, huh?

Right you are!
I think my needles are wilting.

Maybe you need some mousse to keep 'em all in place.

Actually a good rain would help as much as anything.

WRITING

Your Assignment

Write a conversation. Like Maya Angelou, you have already chosen two people (real or imaginary) for the dialogue. Decide on a purpose for their conversation (like convincing Marguerite to talk). Then put them in a setting (like Miss Flowers' house). Finally, let them talk to one another. As you write, change paragraphs whenever you change the person who is talking.

Thinking About the Model

You can show who is speaking without saying "Mrs. Flowers said" or "Momma said." Angelou seldom includes words like "Mrs. Flowers said" in the latter part of the piece. But still, you can tell who's talking.

Paragraphing in dialogue helps you figure it out. Consider these paragraphs from later in the story:

> "How do you like that?"
> It occurred to me that she expected a response. . . .
> I said, "Yes, ma'am." It was the least I could do, but it was the most also.
> "There's one more thing. Take this book of poems and memorize one for me. . . ."

In the first line, it is Mrs. Flowers speaking. Then you read "I said," followed by Marguerite's words. Even though there are no identifying words, we know that Mrs. Flowers speaks the next lines. How? Because a new paragraph begins.

Also, note that in every bit of dialogue, Angelou adds a detail to explain her main idea. In that way, every **part leads to the total.**

As you write your first draft, use a conversation map to help you remember to start a new paragraph every time the speaker changes. Make sure every **part leads to the total.**

Writing Process Tip: Forming Implied Topic Sentences

Sometimes writers do not include a topic sentence in each paragraph. Often you will not find the big-topic sentence in a long piece, especially one like Maya Angelou's conversation. Still, Angelou had a topic, a purpose, and an audience in mind as she wrote. These helped her decide which details to include.

From reading those details, you know her purpose. You can also guess her topic sentence. What do you think her **implied big-topic sentence** is?

In your learning log, write your own big-topic sentence. True, it may not appear in the conversation you write. Still, you must be able to put your big-topic idea into words.

Model your sentence after Angelou's implied big-topic sentence:

> Because Mrs. Flowers is a caring, helpful, gentle lady, Marguerite admires and respects her.

Now Write

Using your prewriting notes, conversation map, and the big-topic sentence, write your first draft of a conversation. Make sure you start a new paragraph each time the speaker changes.

When you finish the first draft, return to the lesson. You will use Angelou's writing as a model to help you revise.

REVISING

Checking Model's Map: The Total and Its Parts in Dialogue

The Maya Angelou piece you read is part of a whole book about her life. Still, this part of the total gives a clear picture of one event in her childhood.

Likewise, every line in a dialogue must somehow lead to the total idea. For instance, every word that Mrs. Flowers speaks has to do with her plan to get Marguerite to speak.

Your own conversation should do the same. Every word that either character says needs to fit your purpose.

Use the following exercise to help you identify the parts of a total.

Exercise A—Identifying the Parts

Directions. In your learning log, number from 1 to 10. Read the following sets of sentences. In each set, one sentence does **not** lead to the writer's purpose. Write the letter of that sentence in your log.

1. words Mrs. Flowers might say because she wants Marguerite to carry her groceries home
   a. "Marguerite is such pleasant company."
   b. "Bailey is such a fine young man."
   c. "I've baked cookies for Marguerite."

2. words Momma might say because she wants Mrs. Flowers to help her daughter
   a. "My Bailey is such a fine, strong young man."
   b. "Marguerite can carry those groceries for you."
   c. "Marguerite reads everything she can find."

3. words Mrs. Flowers might say to get Marguerite to talk
   a. "You can have all the cookies you want."
   b. "The sound of language makes us different from animals."
   c. "Words can change meaning by how they're spoken."

4. words Mrs. Flowers might say to be kind to Marguerite
   a. "You can have more lemonade if you wish."
   b. "The cookies are for you."
   c. "I haven't baked in awhile."

5. details to show that Marguerite likes Mrs. Flowers
   a. I couldn't have said no to her no matter what.
   b. I hung on every word she said.
   c. I wonder why Momma sent me with her.

6. details to show that Marguerite likes her mother
   a. I saw that grown-up look Momma and Mrs. Flowers exchanged.
   b. Momma smiled down at me and sent me to change my dress.
   c. Mrs. Flowers called Momma "Mrs. Henderson," and it made Momma sound so pretty.

7. words Brother Bailey might say to show he understands Marguerite

   a. "Why the devil don't you just say something?"

   b. "I borrowed these books for you to read."

   c. "Momma really wants you to visit Mrs. Flowers."

8. words that Marguerite might say to herself to show she trusts Mrs. Flowers

   a. I thought her cookies would be as perfect as she is.

   b. I wanted to gobble down handfuls of cookies, but Mrs. Flowers wouldn't approve of bad manners.

   c. If Mrs. Flowers wanted me to read aloud, the least I could do was agree.

9. words that Momma might say to get Marguerite to talk

   a. "You can't go through life without talking to people."

   b. "You can't go through life just reading all the time."

   c. "You can't go through life delivering groceries."

10. words that Momma might say to Mrs. Flowers to share her joy when Marguerite finally talks

    a. "Marguerite read aloud last night—I heard her in her room!"

    b. "Marguerite's voice is music to my ears!"

    c. "Marguerite can carry your groceries home."

Exercise B—Identifying the Total from the Parts

Directions. In your learning log, number from 1 to 10. Read the sets of sentences below. Decide on their total purpose. Write the total in your learning log. The first is done for you. (Many correct answers are possible.)

1. a. Marguerite's voice was music to my ears.

   b. The words brought tears to my eyes.

   c. This is the answer to my prayers.

   > Total: Momma is happy that Marguerite is beginning to speak again.

2. a. Words have more meaning than print allows.

   b. The voice gives added meaning.

   c. How you say a word shows how you feel.

3. *a.* Grown-ups exchange looks.

  b. We don't always know what the looks mean.

  c. Maybe they are some kind of code.

4. *a.* Bailey borrowed books for Marguerite to read.

  b. He talked to her often, even though she didn't answer.

  c. He never scolded her for not talking.

5. *a.* Momma ran a neighborhood store.

  b. She stocked basic grocery items.

  c. Since she knew the neighbors, she knew their needs.

6. *a.* Marguerite dressed like all the girls in her neighborhood.

  b. Girls at that time always wore dresses.

  c. Marguerite changed dresses to go to Mrs. Flowers' house.

7. *a.* Mrs. Flowers had prepared cookies and lemonade.

  b. Mrs. Flowers and Momma exchanged grown-up looks.

  c. Mrs. Flowers asks for Marguerite to carry her groceries.

8. *a.* Birds talk in song.

  b. Dogs bark, whine, and growl.

  c. But people talk in words and sentences.

9. *a.* As Mrs. Flowers asked, Marguerite found a poem she liked.

  b. She memorized it.

  c. Then, as she recited it, her voice added meaning to the words.

10. *a.* Mrs. Flowers never laughed.

  b. But she smiled often.

  c. She was a warm, caring gentlewoman.

COMPUTER

Use an on-line thesaurus to help you find other, more powerful words for the common tag verbs like *said, replied, asked,* and *answered.* Then compare your on-line thesaurus with a print thesaurus. Is one better than the other for this purpose? Why or why not?

HINT

Exercise C—Writing Parts to Fit the Total

Directions. See the five pictures on pages 132–133. Pick a character in one picture to talk to a character in the other. Think of a purpose for their conversation.

Write a purpose sentence in your learning log. Write ten sentences of dialogue—five sentences for each character.

Writing a Conversation

Be sure each part of the dialogue supports the total purpose.

Checking the Links: Tags in Dialogue

Words like "she said" or "said Bailey" are called *tags.* Writers use them, along with paragraphing, to show who's talking. But good writers avoid "he said" "she said" repetition.

Review Angelou's writing. Note the tags she uses. Note, too, that she uses few of them.

Likewise, you may be able to avoid dull writing by using paragraphing and a variety of tags.

The following exercises will help you use good tags.

Exercise D—Variety in Tags

Directions. With a partner, make a list of 15 tags. Use a different verb for each. Write them in your learning log. The first three are done for you.

1. she exclaimed
2. shouted Rodney
3. Jessica whimpered

Exercise E—Using Tags

Directions. In your learning log, number from 1 to 10. Refer to your log entries for Exercise D, and add tags in the blank spaces. Try for variety.

1. "How can I help?" _____.
2. "You can carry my groceries," _____.
3. "How about some lemonade," _____, "with those cookies?"
4. "Yes," _____, "I would like some. Thank you."
5. "Well, Marguerite," _____, "I baked these cookies just for you."
6. _____, "I haven't baked in a long time."
7. _____, "We need to have a little chat."
8. "This beautiful language of ours is meant to be heard!" _____.
9. "I want you to promise," _____, "that you will read these books aloud."

10. "And," _____, "I want you to find a poem you like, memorize it, and recite it to me."

Exercise F—Adding Paragraphing

Directions. The following conversation is written as one paragraph. In your learning log, revise the paragraphing to make clear the change of speakers.

When Marguerite walked home with Mrs. Flowers, she was thrilled to be with this great lady. "I am in awe of her," Marguerite said to herself. "Well, now, Marguerite," Mrs. Flowers began, "I understand you're doing very well in school. But your teachers say you don't talk." "That's right," I said to myself. "I don't talk at school or anywhere else." And to prove the point, I remained silent. "You know," Mrs. Flowers continued, "our language is full of meaning that we add with our voices." "I never thought about that before," I said to myself, "but I'm not sure I understand. Maybe she'll explain." "Let me explain. Depending on how you say, 'I'm glad to see you,' you can make it sound just barely polite or really exciting. The written word has no sound. You have to add that." I thought, "What she's saying is beginning to make sense."

Exercise G—Studying Other Dialogue

Directions. Find a short story or other work that includes dialogue. With a partner, choose a page on which the speaker changes at least six times. Make a copy of it to share with the class. Point out how the writer changes paragraphs.

Peer-editor Activity. Ask a peer to check your work for paragraphing. Make any needed revisions.

PROOFREADING

Right Reading: Punctuating Dialogue

Two punctuation rules apply to writing dialogue. Study these rules and the examples.

1. Each tag is set off with punctuation. It will have a comma before it (unless it's at the beginning of a sentence) and a comma or period after it.

    > EXAMPLES: "I'll call her," Momma replied, "and have her help." (comma before and after the tag *Momma replied*)
    >
    > "I'd like Marguerite to carry my bags," Mrs. Flowers said. (comma before and period after the tag)
    >
    > Mrs. Flowers continued, "I want to have a chat with her." (comma after the tag)

2. Put commas and periods inside quotation marks.

    > EXAMPLE: "I'll call her," Momma replied. "She can help you."

Use the following exercises to practice punctuating dialogue.

Exercise H—Finding Errors in Punctuating Dialogue

Directions. In your learning log, number from 1 to 10. There is one punctuation error in each of these sentences. Find it, and explain in your log how to correct it.

1. Maya Angelou wrote "I don't think I ever saw Mrs. Flowers laugh."
2. "But" Angelou continued, "she smiled often."
3. "She was," Angelou recalled "one of the few gentlewomen I have ever known."
4. "Mrs. Flowers has remained my idol" Angelou wrote.
5. She continued, "Mrs. Flowers is the measure of what a human being can be".

SPELLING TIP

Sometimes words in dialogue are spelled in such a way as to reflect the speaker's dialect or pronunciation. If you use other than accepted spellings for that purpose, be sure to note these misspellings to your peer editors and teacher.

Writing: An Art- and Literature-Based Approach

6. As Angelou writes of her childhood, she says "Speaking to Mrs. Flowers was the least I could do."

7. "Likewise", she added, "it was the most also."

8. When young Marguerite began reading aloud, she spoke softly "It was the best of times and the worst of times."

9. "Read these opening lines" Mrs. Flowers commanded.

10. "These lines are from *A Tale of Two Cities*".

Exercise I—Adding Punctuation

Directions. In your learning log, number from 1 to 10. Copy the following sentences and add all necessary punctuation.

1. Momma asked What do you think will help Marguerite talk again?

2. Mrs. Flowers thought and then answered "Let me have a chat with her.

3. What will you talk about Momma asked

4. I've talked and talked to her till I'm blue in the face Momma continued, shaking her head. Nothing helps.

5. Mrs. Flowers smiled and said I'll try something different.

6. What can I do to help Momma asked Just tell me and I'll start right now.

7. First Mrs. Flowers began let's make plans for me to take her to my house.

8. How Momma asked.

9. Why not have her carry my groceries home. I'll have some cookies ready.

10. That's easy enough. I'll call her now.

Peer-editor Activity. Ask a peer to proofread your draft for punctuation. Make any needed revisions.

Final Draft

Prepare a final draft, making revisions and proofreading corrections. Use good form: Indent for new paragraphs. Add a creative title.

If you are doing your final draft at the computer, you can't disguise the order of punctuation marks the way you can in handwritten work. So be sure to put them in the right order. Here are the rules:

1. Put periods and commas inside quotation marks.
2. Put semicolons outside quotation marks.
3. Put question marks and exclamation marks inside quotation marks if they are part of the quotation.
4. Put them outside quotation marks if the whole sentence is a question or exclamation.

For example,
   Mrs. Flowers asked, "Can Marguerite carry my bags, please?"
   Did Mrs. Flowers say, "Marguerite can walk home with me"?

HINT

Peer/Self-editing Chart

Use the following questions to check your final draft.

1. Did my conversation have a clear purpose?
2. Did every part of the conversation help my readers see the purpose?
3. Did I use good paragraphing to help my readers follow the conversation?
4. Are the tags clear but not repetitive?
5. Did I use the right punctuation and capitalization?

Make any final corrections to your conversation before you share it with your audience.

SHARING

To share your conversation, ask peers to read your dialogue. You be the narrator. Practice together so that you all read with expression. Give your oral presentation to the class.

Portfolio Pointers

Put your final draft in your portfolio. Then, on a separate sheet of paper, answer the following questions:

1. What did this writing assignment teach me about writing dialogue?
2. What does this paper show about my progress?
3. What did I do especially well in this paper?
4. What was most difficult for me, and how did I overcome it?

Relating Your Writing to the Workplace: Dialogue with the Boss

You learned earlier that writing changes with audience. Conversation changes with audience, too. You don't talk to your teacher or coach the way you talk to your best friend. Vocabulary changes. Topics change. Tone of voice may change.

Likewise, in the workplace, you won't talk to your boss the way you talk to your co-workers.

Talk with people who do different jobs. Ask them how they talk with their bosses. Are there things they don't talk about? Does age difference affect conversation? Gender? Kind of job? Does the way they talk to their immediate boss differ from the way they talk with someone higher up?

Discuss with the class what you learn.

Check the Atlas

On a map, locate the state of Arkansas. Then find Stamps, the town in which Maya Angelou was living when she walked home with Mrs. Flowers. Later, Angelou moved to St. Louis, Missouri. Locate that city. Which states would she have crossed to go from Stamps to St. Louis?

Interdisciplinary Interest Project: Poetry of the Presidential Inaugurations

President Bill Clinton invited Maya Angelou to write and read a poem for his first inauguration. Titled "On the Pulse of Morning," the poem made a deep impression on the nation as Angelou read the words on January 20, 1993. Other presidents have had poets read at their inaugurations, too. John F. Kennedy, for instance, invited Robert Frost to read at his inauguration.

Get a copy of "On the Pulse of Morning" as well as other poems written for or read at a Presidential Inauguration. Read them aloud in class. Watch a video of a Presidential Inauguration in which a poet shares his or her work. As a class, discuss why you think poets are often included in the ceremony. How does the poetry affect the event?

chapter 9

Giving

Personality to the Wind

PREWRITING

Visuals

1. "Young Woman in a Summer Shower" by Suzuki Haranobu
2. "Yellowstone Lake, Yellowstone National Park" by Ansel Adams
3. "Sand Hills near Abiquin, New Mexico" by Ernest Knee
4. "Monolith" by Willard van Dyke
5. "Stoops in Snow" by Martin Lewis

> *"A cruel snow-laden wind blowing straight out of the pages of Russian history and literature whipped across roofs and through the frozen streets of Moscow."*
> Clifton Daniel, quoted by G. Talese
> *The Kingdom and the Power*

Your Viewer's Response

The wind has many moods, from a kite-flying breeze to a hurricane. Choose one of the pictures. Or choose one from another source. In the picture, what personality does the wind have? In your learning log, list 5 or 6 words or groups of words to describe it.

> EXAMPLES: whipping wind
>
> wind dancing like a boxer in round one
>
> wind skipping on tiptoes

Young Woman in a Summer Shower
by Suzuki Haranobu

Stoops in Snow by Martin Lewis

Sand Hills near Abiquin, New Mexico by Ernest Knee

Yellowstone Lake, Yellowstone National Park
by Ansel Adams

Monolith by Willard Van Dyke

S P E L L I N G
T I P

You are already familiar with certain homonyms: *to, too, two; their, there, they're; sale, sail,* and so on. With your class, make a list of other, less common homonyms, like *pride* and *pried.* Use each in a sentence to show its meaning.

Reading the Literature

The selection you are about to read gives personality to the wind. To do that, the writer uses **strong verbs** to let you see, hear, and feel the wind.

About the Author

Ann Petry (1908–) moved to New York City as a young African-American woman in search of a new life. Her best-known book, *The Street*, is set in that huge, populated sprawl.

Vocabulary

assault (uh SAWLT) n. violent attack

barrage (buh RAHZH) n. a heavy, long-lasting blast

areaways (ER ee uh wayz) n. sunken places that let light or air into a cellar

grime (GRIM) n. sooty dirt

entangling (en TAN guhl ing) v. twisting around, catching, as with a vine

dislodge (dis LAHJ) v. free or loosen

pried (PRID) v. forced, as if with a tool like a crowbar or lever

Excerpt From

THE STREET
by Ann Petry

There was a cold November wind blowing through 116th Street. It rattled the tops of garbage cans, sucked window shades out through the top of opened windows and set them flapping back against the windows; and it drove most of the people off the street in the block between Seventh and Eighth Avenues except for a few hurried pedestrians who bent double in an effort to offer the least possible exposed surface to its violent assault.

Writing: An Art- and Literature-Based Approach

It found every scrap of paper along the street—theater throwaways, announcements of dances and lodge meetings, the heavy waxed paper that loaves of bread had been wrapped in, the thinner waxed paper that had enclosed sandwiches, old envelopes, newspapers. Fingering its way along the curb, the wind set the bits of paper to dancing high in the air, so that a barrage of paper swirled into the faces of the people on the street. It even took time to rush into doorways and areaways and find chicken bones and pork-chop bones and pushed them along the curb.

It did everything it could to discourage the people walking along the street. It found all the dirt and dust and grime on the sidewalk and lifted it up so that the dirt got into their noses, making it difficult to breathe; the dust got into their eyes and blinded them; and the grit stung their skins. It wrapped newspaper around their feet entangling them until the people cursed deep in their throats, stamped their feet, kicked at the paper. The wind blew it back again and again until they were forced to stoop and dislodge the paper with their hands. And then the wind grabbed their hats, pried their scarves from around their necks, stuck its fingers inside their coat collars, blew their coats away from their bodies.

COMPUTER

If your word processing software includes a thesaurus, use it to find synonyms. Remember to check cross references. Usually, you can click on a synonym to find even more words.

Some CD-ROM reference works include a thesaurus. You may also want to explore there.

HINT

Your Reader's Response

Wind can be gentle—just a light breeze. It can also be violent—as in a killer hurricane. What windy experience can you share? Respond in your learning log.

Springboards for Writing

These activities will help you think about the wind.

Individual Activity. Use a thesaurus to look up "wind." Find as many synonyms as you can. Remember to cross reference. For instance, if "breeze" is a synonym, also look it up for more synonyms.

Then, in a sequence chart, arrange the synonyms by meaning. Put the words that mean the least windy to the left. Add words to the right that show the wind as stronger, and finally strongest. Continue to the second or third row as needed to list all your synonyms.

SEQUENCE CHART

Least windy

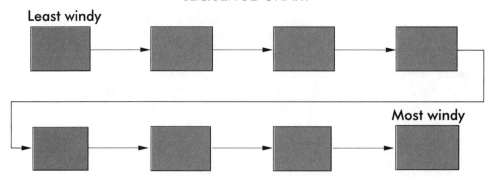

Most windy

Group Activity. In a small group, brainstorm for ways to give the wind personality. For instance, sometimes it's like a carpenter hammering on the windows. Sometimes it's like a madman ripping limbs from the trees. Sometimes it's like a mother soothing a child.

Use sameness charts to show how the wind is like different kinds of people. Think of at least four personalities.

SAMENESS CHART

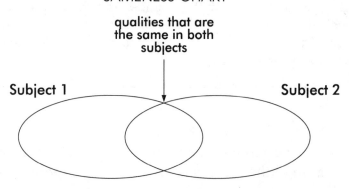

Share your charts in a bulletin board display. Group the charts according to the strength of the wind.

Now Decide

From your Viewer's Response, Reader's Response, or the activities above, pick a personality you want to give to the wind. Write one sentence in your learning log to name the personality. (e.g. "Sometimes the wind is like a madman.")

Studying the Model: Strong Verbs

Ann Petry makes the wind fierce and unfriendly. She does that by using **strong verbs.** All of her verbs are fierce and unfriendly.

Look, for instance, at the second sentence of her work:

> It *rattled* the tops of garbage cans, *sucked* window shades out through the top of opened windows and *set* them flapping back against the windows; and it *drove* most of the people off the street. . . .

If you rewrote that sentence to make the wind less fierce and more friendly, it might read like this:

> It *puffed* at the tops of garbage cans, *tugged* at window shades through the top of opened windows, and *let* them bounce lightly against the windows; and it *slid* across the shoulders and bare heads of the people on the street.

Good writing comes in large part from using a good vocabulary, including strong verbs.

With a partner, make a list of Petry's other strong verbs. As a class, try rewriting her sentences to make the verbs less fierce and more friendly. Try several rewrites to see how verb choice changes the meaning.

Mapping Your Writing: Plan with a Cause-and-Effect Frame

One way to come up with strong verbs is to fill out a cause-and-effect frame. In this case, the wind is the cause. Now, what are its effects?

For instance, does it
    tear leaves from the trees?
    rattle the door?
    roar around the corner?
    whisper across the water?
    sing a sad melody?
    rustle the dry grasses?
    murmur through the sound-proof walls?
    push people across the street?

Each of these is an effect of the wind.

Think about the personality you want to give the wind. What effect would the personality have? In your learning

COMPUTER

If you are using a computer, enter Petry's text. Use the editing tools to copy and paste the passage several times. Then you can delete her verbs and insert your own without rewriting the entire text.

HINT

log, put your responses in one of the cause-and-effect frames.

CAUSE-AND-EFFECT FRAMES

When one cause has several effects

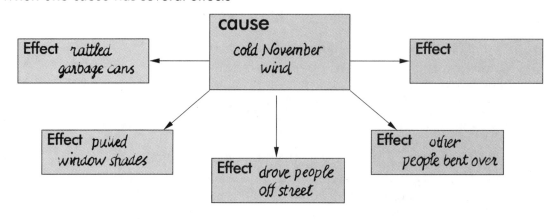

When an effect causes more effects

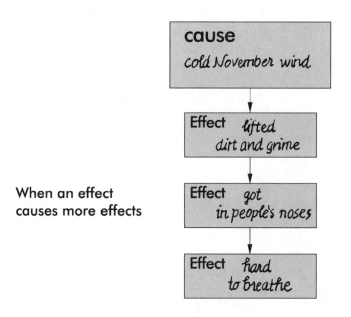

WRITING

Your Assignment

Write a piece in which you give personality to the wind. Choose a location (like Ann Petry's New York City street) and tell about the wind. Wherever possible, give it human characteristics. Use strong verbs to show action, just as Petry did.

Writing: An Art- and Literature-Based Approach

Thinking About the Model

The **strong verbs** that Petry uses are action verbs that are in active voice.

Action verbs (as opposed to linking verbs) do what they say. They show action. For example:

> The day *was* windy. (*Was* is a linking verb. It links the subject *day* to the predicate word *windy*.)

> The wind *blew* all day. (*Blew* shows action and is, therefore, an action verb.)

Active-voice verbs (as opposed to passive-voice verbs) show what the subject is doing. For example:

> People *were pushed* by the wind. (*Were pushed* is passive voice. The subject *people* is being acted upon.)

> The wind *pushed* the people. (*Pushed* is in active voice. The subject *wind* is doing the pushing.)

In addition, her verbs make clear a **cause and effect.** She shows how the wind affects people and places.

Review your cause-and-effect frame. Most of your verbs are probably action verbs in active voice. Like Petry, use these kinds of verbs as you write.

Writing Process Tip: Writing Concluding Sentences

Every paragraph and every larger piece of writing needs to come to an end. Your readers must feel that you have done more than just quit. They must know three things:

> —that you have thought
> through all the parts of
> your topic
> —that you have put all the parts together for them
> —that you have finished what you have to say

Most paragraphs have a **concluding sentence.** It may be a summary or a final statement. Look at Ann Petry's last paragraph. The first sentence is her topic sentence:

COMPUTER

Some writing-program software includes word bins to help you choose strong words—nouns, verbs, adjectives, and adverbs. Check yours for possible help.

HINT

[The wind] did everything it could to discourage the people walking along the street.

All the other sentences show how the wind discouraged people. Then the last sentence shows a final frustrating example. The wind pulls their hats, scarves, and even their coats away from their bodies. You know there's nothing else for the wind to do to discourage people. It's a final, concluding sentence.

Make sure your own writing has a concluding sentence.

Now Write

Using your cause-and-effect frames, write the first draft of your paper. Use strong verbs. Make sure you use the same personality for the wind throughout your paper. End with a sentence that concludes your topic sentence.

When you finish the first draft, return to the lesson. You will use Petry's writing as a model to help you revise.

REVISING

Checking Model's Map: Organizing to Show Cause and Effect

Causes obviously come before effects. In your writing, though, you may be leading readers to the cause of a problem or situation. If so, you may write first about all the effects. On the other hand, like Petry, you may know your readers understand the cause. You are then leading them to think about the effects.

Use a cause-and-effect frame to map Petry's writing.

Next, use the following exercises to apply what you've learned about showing cause and effect.

Exercise A—Identifying Causes and Effects

Directions. In your learning log, number from 1 to 10. Look at the pairs of words below. One is the cause of the other. If the first is the cause of the second, write "cause" in your log. If the first is the effect of the second, write "effect" in your log. The first one is done for you.

1. wind—scraps of paper swirling [cause]

2. trash from gutter swirling—dust in people's eyes

3. people's coats pulled away from their bodies—walking into the wind

4. chicken bones pushed along the curb—areaways cleaned out

5. dust in their eyes—people blinded

6. grit flying in the air—people's skin stung

7. people kicked at the paper—wind wrapped paper around their feet

8. wind wrapped paper around their feet—people had to reach down and pull it off

9. paper swirled high in air—paper hit faces

10. wind grabbed hats and coats—people driven from street

Exercise B—Naming Effects

Directions. In your learning log, number from 1 to 10. Look at the list of causes below. What effects might they have? Write at least one effect for each of these causes. Remember to begin with a strong verb. The first is done for you.

1. strong wind [whip coats away from people's bodies]
2. tornado
3. mild breeze
4. thunderstorm
5. windless fog
6. ice storm
7. blizzard
8. sand storm
9. dust storm
10. whirlwind

Exercise C—Naming Causes

Directions. In your learning log, number from 1 to 10. Look at the list of effects below. What weather and wind causes might they have? Write at least one cause for each of the effects. Use specific nouns. The first is done for you.

1. frosty autumn leaves piled against fences [arctic blast]

2. gaping hole in the roof
3. awnings ripped off the store front
4. leaves dropping, hanging still
5. bare, crooked fingers of limbs scratching the window
6. icicles dripping sideways
7. spider web hanging wet with dew
8. oak leaves rustling dead on the trees
9. pine needles driven into the screened windows
10. snow swirling across the road

Exercise D—Writing Causes and Effects

Directions. In your learning log, number from 1 to 10. Study the five pictures on pages 152–153. Write one sentence about a cause in each. Then write one sentence about an effect in each.

> EXAMPLES: 1. A summer shower caused her to grab laundry from the line. (cause)
> 2. She lost a shoe in the dash. (effect)

Checking the Links: Showing Relationships Among Ideas

Ann Petry lets you see the relationship between the wind and its effects. She does this by using links. In her third paragraph, for instance, she tells how the wind discouraged people on the street:

> It [the wind] found all the dirt and dust and grime
> on the sidewalk and lifted it up
>   *so that* the dirt got into their noses,
>   *making* it difficult to breathe;
> the dust got into their eyes
>   *and* blinded them. . . .
> It wrapped newspaper around their feet
>   *entangling* them
>   *until* the people cursed. . . .

The italicized words above help show the cause-effect relationships among Petry's ideas. Words and phrases such as *so that, and,* and *until* clearly name effects.

Words ending in *-ing*, called present participles, work like adjectives. They describe nouns. So they, too, show effects.

Other words that help show cause-effect relationships include these:

thus	consequently
therefore	following
as a result	resulting
then	next
afterward	after
because	before
since	accordingly
so	so that

The following exercises provide you with practice using links to show relationships.

Exercise E—Adding Links

Directions. In your learning log, number from 1 to 10. Add a good linking word to the following sentences. Use any linking word from the Checking the Links list but use each word only once. The first one is done for you.

1. The wind yanked people's coats away <u>so that</u> the cold reached their very bones.
2. Every scrap of paper was airborne. _____ the streets were swept clean—until the wind stopped.
3. The wind made outdoor life miserable; _____, people felt driven from the streets.
4. The wind was thorough, _____ it fingered every scrap in every doorway and along every curb.
5. _____ the grit and dirt swirled in the air, people were blinded.
6. First they were blinded and _____ they were chilled through and through.
7. _____ if folks had a choice, they left the wind and grime and huddled in their homes.
8. The wind was especially strong that day; _____, even pork chops and chicken bones were pushed along the curb.

9. The _____ mood of the people was one of grumpiness, angry at the misery, kicking at the mess of it.
10. _____, when the wind quit, debris was piled into corners where the wind had lifted it and set it down again.

Exercise F—Checking Linking Words

Directions. Before you wrote your first draft, you completed a cause-and-effect frame. Review it now. Have you used words in your paper to link causes and effects as you show them in your frame? Revise to show better cause-effect relationships.

Peer-editor Activity. Ask a peer to read your paper and suggest at least one place where you can add another link and another strong verb.

PROOFREADING

Right Reading: Verb Tenses

Petry uses strong verbs throughout her writing. She also uses verb tense to show time. Effects, of course, naturally appear in time after the cause.

Because the tense of a verb shows time, you have to use the same tense to show the same time. Only when time changes should you change tense. Look how Petry does it:

> [The wind] *rattled* . . . garbage cans . . .
> *sucked* window shades . . .
> *set* them flapping . . . and it
> *drove* people off the street . . .
>   except for a few . . .
>   pedestrians who
> *bent* double . . .

Every verb is in past tense. Everything in the passage takes place at the same time, so Petry uses the same tense.

The logic to verb tense is simple. Check the time-sense chart on pg. 165.

Follow the same idea in your own writing.

Use the following exercise to see if you can find and correct shifts in verb tense.

Writing: An Art- and Literature-Based Approach

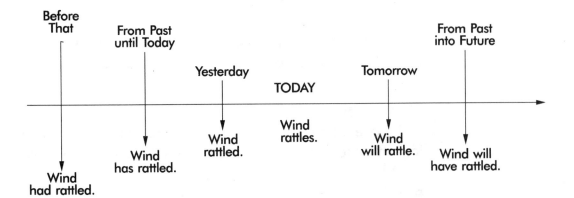

Exercise G—Identifying Shifts in Verb Tense

Directions. In your learning log, number from 1 to 10. Read the following sentences. Each has a verb tense that is illogical. Improve it by writing the correct verb form in your log. (Note that there may be more than one way to correct the shift.) The first one is done for you.

1. As the day wore on, the wind will pick up.

    Corrected: As the day wore on, the wind picked up.

    Or: As the day wears on, the wind will pick up.

2. After the wind quit blowing, people go back out on the street.

3. While the wind howled through the alley, paper flies up above their heads.

4. By the next day, all is calm.

5. By this time next week, all will be calm for long enough to forget its present violence.

6. Having seen the strong wind gusts, people had been pleased to find their roofs still in place.

7. Tomorrow's calm seemed surreal.

8. Until they clean the streets of debris, evidence of the storm remained.

9. Windows and doors, loose in their casings, had rattled before but never like they are now.

Giving Personality to the Wind

10. Won't a toasty fire in the fireplace feel good on a night like that?

Peer-editor Activity. Ask a peer to read your paper and check for logical verb tense. Revise as needed.

Final Draft

Prepare a final draft, making revisions and proofreading corrections. Use good form. Add a "personality" title.

Peer/Self-editing Chart

Use the following questions to check your final draft.

1. Did I give the wind a clear personality?
2. Do all of the details reflect the same personality?
3. Did I use strong action verbs in active voice?
4. Did I use clear cause-effect links?
5. Did I use logical verb tense?
6. Does the paper have a conclusion?

Make final corrections to your paper before you share it with your audience.

CAPITALIZATION TIP

As you proofread, also check capitalization. Personified nouns are often capitalized. Check these examples against your own writing:

Old Man Winter raged through the streets.

Autumn colors are Mother Nature's gift.

No one can stop Father Time on his march.

SHARING

Sometimes the wind makes a lot of noise. As you prepare to share your work, think about the sounds your words suggest. Make a tape recording of your work. Add a few good sound effects. Play your tape for the class.

Portfolio Pointers

Put your final draft into your portfolio. Then, on a separate sheet of paper, answer the following questions:

1. What writing strengths does this paper show?
2. What was hard for me, and how did I overcome that?
3. What did I learn that I can use on another writing task?
4. What did I learn from someone else about writing as I worked on this piece?

Writing: An Art- and Literature-Based Approach

Relating Your Writing to the Workplace: Telephone Personality

You've given the wind personality. Like the unseen wind, the unseen voice on the telephone shows a personality. For instance, think about the many ways you've heard "hello." Some voices sound happy, sad, angry, or cheerful. Some voices seem to have a smile.

In the workplace, a pleasant telephone voice and good telephone manners can help business. In this age of answering machines and voice mail, a "smiling" voice is even more important. As a class, make a list of specific traits a good telephone personality should have. How would it sound? What would it say?

Check the Atlas

The Street is set in New York City. On a United States map, locate New York State and New York City. Next, find a New York City map. Trace 116th Street. Which direction does it run? In what part of the city is it?

Interdisciplinary Interest Project: Cause of the Wind and Its Effects

Do you know what causes the wind? Do you know why some winds are so violent that they cause destruction—even death? What would happen if we never had any wind?

Research the cause of wind. Prepare a brief report in which you answer some of the questions above as well as others you and your classmates have.

Internet Connection

AccuWeather at http://accuwx.com. is one of the best-known commercial weather services. Use some of the graphics here to add pizzazz to your report.

Another site of interest is the Weather Channel at http://www.weather.com.

chapter 10

Writing

a Travel Piece

PREWRITING

Visuals

1. "Hyéres, France" by Henri Cartier-Bresson
2. "Earth and Water" by Rebecca Salsbury James
3. "Highway and Mesa" by Woody Gwyn
4. "The Coast of Labrador" by William Bradford
5. "Gondor Market: Ethiopian Mother" by John Biggers

> *"Traveling is not just seeing the new; it is also leaving behind."*
>
> Jan Martial, author
> *The Silk Road*

Your Viewer's Response

Choose a picture that reminds you of a place you think others should visit, such as your city or town, a museum, ballpark, or vacation spot. In your learning log, name the spot. Then list three reasons that you think others should travel there.

EXAMPLE: Travel to   because
our state capital   1. pretty build-
                        ings, gardens,
                        lights at night
                    2. great history
                        in monu-

Gondor Market: Ethiopian Mother
by John Biggers

Hyéres, France by Henri Cartier-Bresson

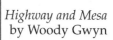

Highway and Mesa
by Woody Gwyn

The Coast of Labrador by William Bradford

Earth and Water by Rebecca Salsbury James

Understanding prefixes helps you understand meanings. It also helps you spell correctly.

Remember that the prefix does not change the spelling of the root word. Check these words:

immensity = im (not) + mensus (measure)

incessantly = in (not) + cessans (cease or stop)

interspersed = inter (among) + spargere (scatter)

ments, on tours

3. fun things nearby

Reading the Literature

The travel piece you are about to read uses **parallelism** to make ideas strong. Watch for two groups of words that have the same grammatical parts, such as "one of the loneliest parts of the United States [and] one of the most awesome."

About the Author

Among the many cultures that Brent Ashabranner has written about, perhaps the Mexican–United States neighborliness is his favorite theme. To make his point, he toured the length of the border and wrote about his experiences.

Vocabulary

immensity (im MEN si tee) n. very large size; hugeness

awesome (AW suhm) adj. causing a feeling of wonder brought about by greatness

arid (AR id) adj. so dry that nothing will grow

incessantly (in SES uhnt li) adv. without stopping

scarcity (SKER suh tee) n. lack

remoteness (ri MOHT nes) n. being far away

immerse (im MERS) v. sink

desolate (DES uh lit) adj. deserted, lonely

interspersed (in tuhr SPERST) adj. scattered here and there

peccaries (PEK uh rees) n. pig-like animals

Excerpt From

I GET AGGRAVATED AND NERVOUS IN TOWN
by Brent Ashabranner

from The Vanishing Border: A Photographic Journey Along Our Frontier with Mexico

The border country between El Paso and Del Rio, 425 miles to the east, must be one of the loneliest parts of the United States. Yet in its immensity, it is surely one of the most awesome. A huge, arid land, tumbleweeds are thick, the wind blows incessantly, and dust devils twist across the empty landscape. Along the highway we passed Fasten Seat Belt signs with bullet holes in them, victims of casual target practice, and roadside picnic areas posted with Beware of Poison Snakes signs.

This is cattle country. For mile after lonely mile only an occasional windmill reminded us that people must live here. Around water holes we saw antelope mixing with cattle. After the urban throb of El Paso and Juárez, the scarcity of people was startling. The few towns along this stretch of the Rio Grande are tiny, none with more than two thousand people. The river is narrow here, the border guarded only by towering mountains on the Mexican side.

Halfway between El Paso and Laredo the Rio Grande changes its southeasterly direction, makes a great U-turn, and flows northeast for a considerable distance. This is the Big Bend, a place of towering mountains and spectacular canyons through which the fast-flowing river winds its way. Since 1944, eleven hundred square miles of mountains and desert within the *U* have been set aside as Big Bend National Park, a great wilderness area.

Despite its remoteness, thousands of visitors come every year to immerse themselves in the desolate beauty of this vast park. Cumulus clouds rest on top of the jagged Chisos Mountains. Shrubs and cacti cover the desert floor, interspersed with crowds of wild flowers during the spring and summer. Canoers paddle through

Many Web sites give information about travel destinations. Some of the more interesting ones in the United States include:

CityNet United States at http://www.city.net

Disneyland at http://www2.disney.com/Disneyland/index.html?GL=H

Mexico: An Endless Journey at http://mexico-travel.com/

National Park Service at http://www.nps.gov

Paperless Guide to NYC at http://www.mediabridge.com/nyc

Seattle, the Emerald City at http://www.seanet.com/Seattle/SeattleHome.html

Universal Studios Hollywood and Florida at http://www.mca.com/unitemp/index.html

You can also find international travel destinations on the Web as well as a series of travel guides.

the deep canyons. The patient watcher can see desert mule deer, coyotes, foxes, peccaries, and, with great luck, perhaps a mountain lion.

For the bird watcher, Big Bend is the nearest thing to heaven. Over three hundred species inhabit its 750,000 acres at different times of the year. Paul is a passionate and totally dedicated bird watcher. One hot July morning, equipped with binoculars and two canteens of water, he set out for Boot Springs, high in the mountains. It is there, and only there in the entire country, that the shy, retiring Colima warbler sometimes can be seen. Just at nightfall when I was becoming concerned, Paul returned, weary, several pounds lighter, but a happy man. He had seen not one Colima warbler but two.

After the gigantic detour of Big Bend, the Rio Grande gets on about its business of reaching the Gulf of Mexico.

Your Reader's Response

Think again about this place you believe others should visit. In your learning log, make a list of details that Ashabranner might want to know about that place.

Springboards for Writing

The following activities will help you think about places that others should visit.

Individual Activity. Make three cluster maps. In the center of the first map, write "Local." In the second, write "Area"; in the third, "Far Away." Then see how many destinations you can list in each.

For instance, for "Local" you might list places within the city or county limits, such as your neighborhood park or museum. In "Area," you might list places within a hundred miles or a day's drive to and from home. Everything else goes in "Far Away."

Share your cluster maps with the class. As each of you shares your map, make a list of all the places you and your classmates think others should visit. Post the list in the classroom.

Group Activity. With two or three peers, look through travel magazines or brochures. You will find many of the same topics in each. One topic may be "things to do."

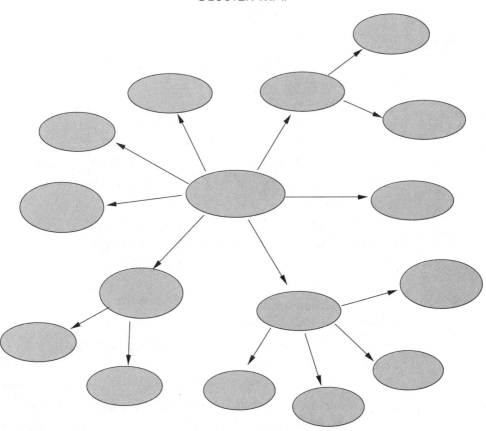

Ashabranner, for instance, talks about birding in Big Bend National Park.

As a group, make a list of the common topics. Then, as a class, compile all the lists. Discuss how many of these topics Ashabranner uses. In your learning log, list the ones that are most important to you.

Studying the Model: Parallel Structures

To give similar ideas a similar sound, good writers like Ashabranner use **parallel structures.** You already know what the word *parallel* means—running side by side like railroad tracks. In language, a parallel structure has the same grammatical form. For instance, look at these pairs of parallel structures from Ashabranner's work:

> around water holes (preposition, object)
> after the urban throb (preposition, object)

> changes its southeasterly direction (verb, object)
> makes a great U-turn (verb, object)

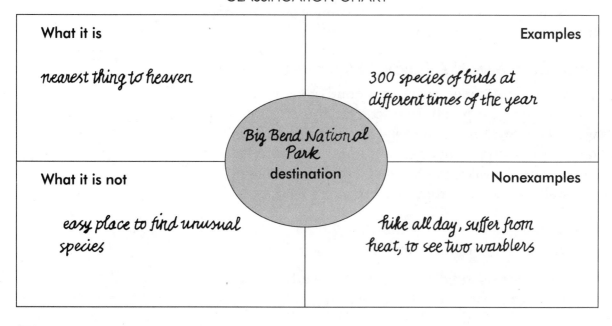

Internet Connection

Travel can be by backpack, boat, bicycle, car, plane, and so on. To get information about some travel destinations, go to the following URL:
http://www.yahoo.com/Recreation/Travel/.
Then ask for "Travelogues, Specific" and type in the destination (for example: Cincinnati).

one of the loneliest (noun, prepositional phrase)
one of the most awesome (noun, prepositional phrase)

Fasten Seat Belt signs with bullet holes (adjective, noun, prepositional phrase)
roadside picnic areas with Beware of Poison Snakes signs (adjective, noun, prepositional phrase)

The parallel structures give the writing a sense of rhythm, like repeated drum beats. The rhythm makes the reading a pleasure.

With a partner, find at least five more parallel structures in Ashabranner's writing. Try to identify the grammar. Share your findings with the class.

Mapping Your Writing: Explore with a Classification Chart

To tell why a place is worth visiting, you need to set it apart from other, similar places.

Use the classification chart to think about what your travel destination is and is not. Next, name examples of what you find there. Finally, list examples of what you would not find there.

These details help you make your travel destination different from others.

CLASSIFICATION CHART

What it is	Examples
nearest thing to heaven	300 species of birds at different times of the year
Big Bend National Park — destination	
What it is not	Nonexamples
easy place to find unusual species	hike all day, suffer from heat, to see two warblers

WRITING

Your Assignment

Write a travel piece. Choose a specific destination like Ashabranner's Big Bend National Park. Explain why it is a good place to visit. Use parallel structures to give strength to ideas.

Thinking About the Model

The logic in Ashabranner's **parallel structures** shows him to be good with language. He uses parallelism to **classify details** in two ways.

First, he puts *opposite* ideas in parallel for emphasis:

> The drive along the border is "one of the loneliest" yet "one of the most awesome."

Putting opposite ideas side by side in the same grammatical form is like dressing twins in different suits. It forces attention on the suits' differences.

Second, Ashabranner puts *similar* ideas in parallel for emphasis, too:

> They pass "Fasten Seat Belt signs with bullet holes in them" and "roadside picnic areas posted with Beware of Poison Snakes signs."

Putting similar ideas side by side in the same grammatical form is like dressing twins in the same suit. It focuses attention on how much the suits—and the twins—really do look alike.

Try to use the same kind of logic in your own parallel structures.

Writing Process Tip: Making the Logic Clear

Your readers must be able to follow your logic. Good links between one idea and the next show your logic. For example:

> *When you travel the Southwest,* you can enjoy snow-capped mountains and desert on the same day. (sentence beginnings)

Several style checkers include "transition checkers." These tools highlight transitions and, in some cases, include word bins with lists of transitions appropriate for the mapping plan you are using. Using this tool, you can work alone or with a peer to revise for logic.

HINT

The Southwest, *unlike the Northwest,* is hot and dry. (likeness-difference words)

Traveling along the Rio Grande is like *traveling* in a time machine. (repetition)

You have studied a different kind of link in each chapter. Review them now:

time-order words   (Chapter 2)
repetition   (Chapter 3)
space-order words   (Chapter 4)
sentence beginnings   (Chapter 5)
step-by-step phrases   (Chapter 6)
likeness-difference words (Chapter 7)
tag lines in dialogue   (Chapter 8)
cause-effect words   (Chapter 9)

As you write your travel piece, use links to **make the logic clear.**

Now Write

Using your classification chart for ideas, write your first draft. Use parallel ideas whenever possible.

When you finish the first draft, return to the lesson. You will use Ashabranner's writing as a model to help you revise.

REVISING

Checking Model's Map: Classifying the Details

Good travel pieces must show you what's there. They usually have four or five main ideas. These may include the following:

—historical places to visit
—sites to see
—places to shop
—best places to eat
—recreation spots
—children's activities

Each of these ideas is explained with details.

Ashabranner classifies details according to where he is along the 425-mile border.

In the first paragraph, he details the drive between El Paso and Del Rio. It's lonely, immense, and awesome. The road signs add caution.

In the second paragraph, he details the cattle country. In the third, he moves to the Big Bend.

Use the chart below to classify Ashabranner's details. You may not need all of the squares.

CLASSIFYING THE DETAILS

	Idea 1 *loveliest part of U.S.*	Idea 2	Idea 3	Idea 4	Idea 5
Detail 1	*immense and awesome*				
Detail 2	*dry, with tumbleweeds*				
Detail 3	*wind never stops; dust devils*				
Detail 4	*highway signs*				

The following exercises will help you practice classifying details.

Exercise A—Classifying Details

Directions. In your learning log, number from 1 to 5. Study the following classifications from Ashabranner's writing. Find at least two details from his writing that fit each classification and write them in your log. The first one is done for you.

1. road signs [Fasten Seat Belt and Beware of Poison Snakes]

2. scarcity of people

3. cattle country
4. desolate beauty of park
5. dedicated bird watchers

Exercise B—Labeling the Classification

Directions. In your learning log, number from 1 to 10. Classify the following details from Ashabranner's writing. Write the classification in your log. The first one is done for you.

1. Fasten Seat Belt, Beware of Poisonous Snakes, No Parking on Roadside [highway signs]
2. windmills, watering troughs, pastures
3. small towns, towns far apart, no border guards
4. tumbleweeds, dust devils, arid land, wind
5. thousands of visitors, canoeists, bird watchers
6. shrubs, cacti, wild flowers
7. mountains, canyons, fast-flowing river
8. desert mule deer, coyotes, foxes, peccaries, mountain lion
9. binoculars, water, hiking boots, bird identification book
10. weary, lighter, happy

Exercise C—Organizing by Classification

Directions. In your learning log, number from 1 to 5. Leave six blank lines for each number. Study the groups of words below. Classify each group by naming a heading and two subheadings. Then arrange the details with their subheadings. The first one is done for you. The second one is partly done.

1. El Paso, Big Bend National Park, Juárez, Del Rio, Rio Grande River, Chisos Mountains

   Main heading: Places to Visit Along the Border
   Two subheadings:

Cities	Natural Wonders
El Paso	Big Bend National Park
Juárez	Rio Grande River
Del Rio	Chisos Mountains

Writing: An Art- and Literature-Based Approach

2. desert mule deer, Colima warbler, coyotes, foxes, peregrine falcon, red-tail hawk

   Main heading: Animals in Big Bend National Park

3. hikers, car-window sightseers, canoeists, mountain climbers, visitors to the visitor center, sunbathers

4. occasional windmill, antelope with cattle, busy markets, throngs of people, heavy traffic, empty landscape

5. wild flowers, shrubs, mountain peaks, cacti, rushing river, cumulus clouds

Exercise D—Writing by Classification

Directions. In your learning log, number from 1 to 30. Study the pictures on pages 170–171. Then answer these questions.

Re: "Hyéres, France"

1–4. Name four details, in addition to "steps," classified by line.

5–6. Name two details that tell about motion in the picture.

Re: "Earth and Water"

7–11. Name five details that can be classified as "nature's objects."

12–13. Name two objects in the foreground.

14–15. Name two objects that can be classified as distant.

Re: "Highway and Mesa"

16–18. Classify three kinds of surfaces in addition to "smooth and flat."

Re: "The Coast of Labrador"

19–21. Classify three kinds of surfaces.

22–23. Name two textures in addition to "wet."

Re: "Gondor Market: Ethiopian Mother"

24–25. Classify two kinds of people in addition to "walking."

26–28. Name three details classified as "curved."

29–30. Name two details in the distance.

Exercise E—Checking Classification Details

Directions. Try using the classifying-the-details chart on page 179 to check your own writing. Does the chart for your writing look something like the chart for Ashabranner's writing? Revise as needed.

Checking the Links: Connecting Parallel Parts

Only a few linking words commonly connect parallel parts. If you review Ashabranner's work, you will see that he uses the common ones: *and, but, yet,* and *or.*

> one of the loneliest *yet* one of the most awesome
> shrubs *and* cacti
> there *and* only there
> weary, lighter, *but* happy
> not one *but* two

Other links sometimes used to join parallel parts include the linking verbs (*is, am, are, was, were, be, been*) and these words and word groups:

also	not	but not
just like	with	along with
still		nevertheless

Sometimes the link is not a word but a punctuation mark. For instance, Ashabranner writes,

> The tumbleweeds are thick, the wind blows incessantly, and dust devils twist across the empty landscape.

> The river is narrow here, the border [is] guarded only by towering mountains.

Note, too, that when Ashabranner moves to another part of his travel piece, he uses linking word groups. Find the paragraphs that begin with the following:

> This is cattle country.
> Halfway between El Paso and Laredo . . .
> Despite its remoteness . . .
> After the gigantic detour of Big Bend . . .

Try to do the same in your own writing. Revise as needed.

The following exercises will give you practice in using connecting words.

Exercise F—Adding Connecting Words

Directions. In your learning log, number from 1 to 10. Add a logical connecting word or word group to these parallel parts.

1. The Mexico–United States border follows the Rio Grande River between the towering mountains _____ a rushing river.

2. It's a land where windmills pump water, tumbleweeds dot the land, _____ people raise cattle.

3. Even though it's a barren land, it's _____ an awesome land.

4. To visit the area _____ to love the place.

5. Seeing a rare bird, spotting a mountain lion, _____ finding a fossil is something to hope for.

6. A rare sighting is something to hope for, _____ it's not something to expect.

7. Only the most patient, persistent, _____ lucky observer will be likely to see a mountain lion.

8. The floor of the desert is decorated with shrubs, the mountain draped with clouds, _____ the river dotted with canoeists.

9. Visitors come for active recreation, restful sightseeing, _____ peaceful camping, but no one comes to sleep.

10. Alongside the mountains, across the desert, _____ near the rushing river wildlife abounds.

Exercise G—Checking Parallel Links

Directions. Reread your draft. Highlight the linking words that connect parallel parts. Can you add any parallel parts? Revise as needed.

Peer-editor Activity. Ask a peer to read your draft for parallel parts. Ask him or her to look for linking words you may have missed.

PUNCTUATION TIP

When three or more words or word groups are written together, they are called a *series*. Use commas to separate items in a series.

The river changes direction, makes a U-turn, and follows the mountain.

COMPUTER

If your text is on a computer file, you can highlight this way. With the mouse, highlight the linking words. Then go to the font menu and click on a different font. For instance, you could use **bold** or *italics* to highlight the linking words. Or you could use a different font type, like this.

HINT

As you proofread, check capitalization. A travel piece may refer to directions, such as north, south, east, and west. When these words name a region, they are capitalized. Compare these two sentences:

Del Rio is 425 miles to the east of El Paso.

We visited the East.

PROOFREADING

Right Reading: Checking Parallelism

Good parallel parts should have the same grammatical forms. In other words, if one of the parallel parts consists of a noun with two adjectives, then the other parallel part should consist of a noun with two adjectives.

Here are some examples of good parallel parts:

The river
—changes direction,
—makes a U-turn, and
—follows the mountain.
(Each parallel part has a verb and an object.)

—After driving three hundred miles,
—after passing many tiny towns, and
—before reaching another big city,
Ashabranner admits he gets nervous in town.
(Each parallel part begins the same way, followed by an -*ing* word, followed by two adjectives and a noun.)

Study Ashabranner's work for other similar grammatical forms.

Use the following exercise to practice correcting poor parallelism.

Exercise H—Correcting Faulty Parallel Parts

Directions. The following sentences have faulty parallel parts. The faulty part is in *italics*. In your learning log, number from 1 to 10. Correct the parallelism.

1. Along the mountain ridges, near the rushing river, or *even cacti in the desert* birds nest and raise young.

2. The floor of the desert is scattered with shrubs, cacti, and *crowded with wild flowers*.

3. Clouds bump into the mountains, gather above the desert, and *the river has them hovering over it*.

4. Bird watchers spend long hours in the sun, through the rain, and *watching until it's almost dark*.

5. Hiking steep mountain trails, trudging flat desert washes, and *to climb rugged ravines* makes for active trips into the park.

6. Windmills pumping water, antelope grazing with cattle, and *people who live in small towns* make up much of the border land.

7. To drive the highway, to visit the towns, and *watching the scenery* is enough for some tourists.

8. Tumbleweeds, rounded by the wind, *that bounce along the road*, and piled against fences are common in the Southwest.

9. Whether you visit there, hike there, or *take a car through there*, the border country has its attraction.

10. The river makes a U-turn, changes direction, and *the current gets faster.*

Peer-editor Activity. Put brackets [like this] around the parallel parts in your paper. Then ask a peer to check the parallel parts for the same grammatical forms. Revise as needed.

Final Draft

Prepare a final draft, making revisions and proofreading corrections. Use good form. Add a title that hints at, but does not name, your destination.

Peer/Self-editing Chart

Use the following questions to check your final draft.

1. Did I show how my travel destination differs from others similar to it?
2. Did I classify my details logically?
3. Are the main ideas and supporting ideas clear?
4. Did I use good parallel parts?
5. Did I use good linking words to join parallel parts?
6. Did I use good linking words or word groups to connect main ideas?

Make final corrections to your travel piece before you share it with your audience.

SHARING

As a class, turn your travel pieces into chapters for a travel booklet. Add maps, drawings or photos, and headings to make an attractive layout.

Then, as a class, mark each destination on a large map.

With the map in the center, make a bulletin board display. Run a piece of string or yarn from each chapter in the booklet to its spot on the map.

Portfolio Pointers

Put your final draft into your portfolio. Then, on a separate sheet of paper, answer the following questions:

1. What am I most pleased with in this paper?
2. What am I least pleased with?
3. If I did this assignment over, what would I do differently?
4. What did I learn from this assignment that I can use in another piece of writing?

Relating Your Writing to the Workplace: Map Skills at Work

Travel is often part of the workplace. Whether the job entails delivering pizzas or running a Fortune 500 company, everyone needs to be able to find an address or a meeting place. Map skills are part of almost any job.

Get a map of your city. Trace the route from the nearest airport to your house. Then write directions for someone at the airport to find your house. Assume that this person has just flown in and has never been to your city or town before.

Check the Atlas

Ashabranner writes about the border between the United States and Mexico. Study a map. Which states border Mexico? How much of the U.S.-Mexico border is defined by the Rio Grande River? Find the cities Ashabranner mentions: El Paso, Del Rio, Juárez, and Laredo.

Then locate other places he mentions: Big Bend National Park, Chisos Mountains, and the Gulf of Mexico. What other cities or towns would Ashabranner have to pass through on his journey along the entire border?

Interdisciplinary Interest Project: Animals Native to the Southwest

Ashabranner mentions animals native to the United States–Mexico border area. Choose one that he mentions or that you know is native to the area. Find out what you can about its habits. Where does it live? What does it eat? How does it raise its young? What are its enemies? How is it equipped to deal with the hot, dry weather?

In a brief report, share what you learn with the class. Include a drawing, illustration, or photograph of the animal.

As a class, create a bulletin board display of all the animals. Be sure to label each picture with the name of the animal. Finally, put the reports together in a booklet available to anyone who sees the bulletin board.

chapter 11

Comparing

Two Places to Live

PREWRITING

Visuals

1. "Ashanti [Ghana] Architecture" by John Biggers
2. "Night Snow at Kambara" by Ando Hiroshige
3. "New York City" by Helen Levitt
4. "Corn Field, Indian Farm near Tuba City, Arizona, in Rain" by Ansel Adams
5. "And the Home of the Brave" by Charles Demuth

"It's a vast, lonely, forbidding expanse of nothing . . . rather like clouds and clouds of pumice stone. And it certainly does not appear to be a very inviting place to live or work."

Frank Borman, U.S. astronaut during first manned orbit of moon

Your Viewer's Response

Choose one of the pictures above. Or choose one from another source.

When you have chosen a picture, ask yourself this question: "What do I think it would be like to live there?" In your learning log, make two columns. Label one "Where I Live Now." Label the other "Compared to _____." List three or four details about each.

Corn Field, Indian Farm near Tuba City,
Arizona, in Rain by Ansel Adams

New York City by Helen Levitt

And the Home of the Brave
by Charles Demuth

Ashanti [Ghana] Architecture by John Biggers

Night Snow at Kambara by Ando Hiroshige

EXAMPLE:

Where I Live Now	Compared to the Country
city has everything easy to get to	have to drive long way to get groceries or anything else
lots of people	few people
no grass to mow	lots of grass and trees, other yard work

Reading the Literature

In the selection you are about to read, Andy Rooney tells you why he loves his big-city home. To explain, he **compares and contrasts** New York City and Toulon, Illinois.

About the Author

As a television journalist, Andrew Rooney (1919–) has worked for CBS, NBC, and PBS. Best known for his witty comments and sly humor, he writes about everyday life.

Vocabulary

brimming (BRIM ming) adj. full to the top edge, as of a cup or bowl

harrowing (HAR oh ing) v. breaking up soil with a harrow, which is a frame with sharp spikes or sharp-edged disks pulled behind a tractor

incredulous (in KREJ oo luhs) adj. skeptical, unbelieving

hedged (HEJD) v. refused to give a direct answer

sentimental (sen tuh MENT l) adj. based more on emotion than on reason

yearn (YERN) v. long for

facilities (fuh SIL uh teez) n. buildings or rooms that make certain activities possible, such as an auditorium or hospital

mingling (MING guhl ing) v. mixing together with; associating with

BIG · CITY BLUES
by Andrew A. Rooney

from *Not That You Asked*

I just spent two days in Toulon. You go there much?

Toulon, Illinois, is 125 miles southwest of Chicago, 40 miles northwest of Peoria and 7 miles from the town of Wyoming. Toulon's population, 1,390. How you feel about where you've been depends partly on luck. If you hit it just right and everything goes smoothly, you leave a place with fond memories. It only takes a flat tire or a bad meal to turn you against a town forever.

I hit Toulon just right. It was a lovely spring day when I got there, with temperatures bordering on summer. Everyone in town was brimming with friendliness, the flowers were blooming, the farmers just outside town were harrowing their fields. All was right with Toulon that day and I found myself wondering why the whole world wasn't headed there to live.

"You have to go back to New York tomorrow?" a native asked, incredulous at the thought of such a dreadful fate. "I was to New York," he said. "Or to New Jersey, anyway, right near New York. I had to meet these people at a motel all right but I was on the wrong side. Road was divided, you know. Took me nearly forty-five minutes to get back over there to meet them. Just maybe fifty feet away and it took me forty-five minutes. Traffic? Man! I sure wouldn't want to live in New York. You like it there?" he asked, challenging me to make a fool of myself by saying I did.

I hedged.

There's a continuing argument about the best places to live in the United States.

There are people who love Florida, people who hate Florida. There are those who wouldn't live anywhere but California. Southerners can't imagine living anywhere but in the South and Midwesterners think anywhere else is something less than 100 percent American.

There are those who love New York and those you couldn't pay enough to live in New York. The biggest argument of all is the argument over whether it's best to live in the big city or the small town. The strange thing is

SPELLING TIP

You know that a spell checker (usually part of word processing software) is a wonderful tool. But watch out! It checks only for spelling, not for correct words. For instance, it cannot tell the difference between *their* and *there*. It only knows that both are spelled correctly. It also cannot recognize keyboarding errors like "The bat frank the bill" when you mean to say "The cat drank the milk." All of the words in both sentences are spelled correctly.

that the fewest people live where most people say they'd like to live; the most people live where most people say they wouldn't want to live.

Everyone talks as though they'd like to live in the country. Everyone loves the small town and the little village, but in spite of all the sentimental talk, the movement is out of the small towns and the country and into the big cities. Those who live in the city yearn for the country but they don't move there.

When you fly over the wide open spaces of America or drive to a small town, it's hard to keep from wondering why the crowded, unhappy, homeless people of the dirty cities don't go to the small towns.

I know there are good reasons. The homeless would still be homeless when they got there and the people already living in town wouldn't welcome them or have the same facilities for helping them that the cities have.

The argument between big-city and small-town life comes down to this: Is it better to fill your life with a wide variety of friends and events in a big city and expose yourself and your family to all the evils that exist there or is it wiser to settle down to the comfortable, the familiar and possibly dull, in a small town? Can you live a fuller life and thus make life seem longer by going places, doing things and mingling with more interesting people in a big city? Or is the quiet continuity of life in a small town more fulfilling?

I loved Toulon, but I'm back in New York by choice.

Your Reader's Response

If you could talk to Andy Rooney about where you live, what would you tell him? In your learning log, make a list of what he would like. To be fair, make another list of what you think he wouldn't like.

Springboards for Writing

Use one or both of the following activities to help you think about two places to compare.

Individual Activity. Imagine you are the mayor of the ideal community. What would you tell businesspeople who might be thinking about moving to your town? Use a double-entry form to plan what you would say. In the left-hand column, make a list of the details you would tell them. In the right-hand column, compare the details with similar details about your hometown.

DOUBLE-ENTRY FORM

Details about Ideal Community	Details about Home Town
1.	1.
2.	2.
3.	3.
4.	4.
5.	5.

Group Activity. In a small group, make plans for a city that meets the needs of everyone. Use a double-entry form like the one above to plan the city. In the left-hand column make a list of needs. In the right-hand column tell how you would meet the needs.

Needs, Ideal City	How to Meet the Needs
1. sanitation	
2. streets	
3.	
4.	
5.	

Draw a plan for the city. Then explain the plan. Include buildings, streets and bridges, a list of services, and so on. Present your ideal city to the class.

As a class, discuss which features make one city better than another.

Now Decide

From your Viewer's Response, Reader's Response, or the activities above, pick two places you want to compare.

COMPUTER

To try different plans for your paper, use the block or select command to move text. Use the mouse to highlight a block of text you want to move. Choose "cut" in the edit menu. Then move the cursor to the place in which you want to insert the text. Choose "paste" in the edit menu.

If the new order seems awkward or illogical, simply repeat the process to move the text back to its original location.

HINT

In your learning log, write one sentence. It should say something such as, "By comparing (one place to live) with (another place to live), I will explain why (this place) is the better place to live."

Studying the Model: Comparisons and Contrasts

Andy Rooney has a way of comparing small towns with New York City that makes you smile.

Comparisons and contrasts have to be easy to follow. So Rooney begins with a little contrast to set you up for a big comparison:

> It only takes a flat tire or a bad meal to turn you against a town forever. I hit Toulon just right.

With his opening contrast, Rooney tells you he had a good experience in Toulon. He also tells what's good about small towns: less traffic, fewer people, friendly people.

But he also tells what's good about large cities: wide variety of friends, lots of events, and a fuller life.

What other comparisons and contrasts do you find? Record them in your learning log.

Mapping Your Writing: Think with a Comparison-Contrast Frame

To help you think about the two places you want to compare, use the comparison-contrast frame on page 197.

First think how the two places are alike. List their similarities in the top part of the frame.

Then think about their differences. For instance, one difference Rooney points out is the traffic. In small towns, you can walk across the road. In large cities, you may have to drive a long way to get across the road.

List as many likenesses and differences for your topic as you can.

WRITING

Your Assignment

Write a piece in which you compare two places to live. Like Andy Rooney, give both sides of the story—the good

PUNCTUATION TIP

Linking words often need commas after them. Study these examples:

By contrast the big city offers excitement.

On the other hand, small towns are often quiet.

They drive tractors in small towns, *not* limos.

The tractors, *however,* cost more than a dozen limos.

Likewise, other farm equipment makes city living look cheap.

Limos, *on the other hand,* are more comfortable riding.

Note that when the words come in the middle of a sentence, you must use a comma before and after them.

Writing: An Art- and Literature-Based Approach

COMPARISON-CONTRAST FRAME

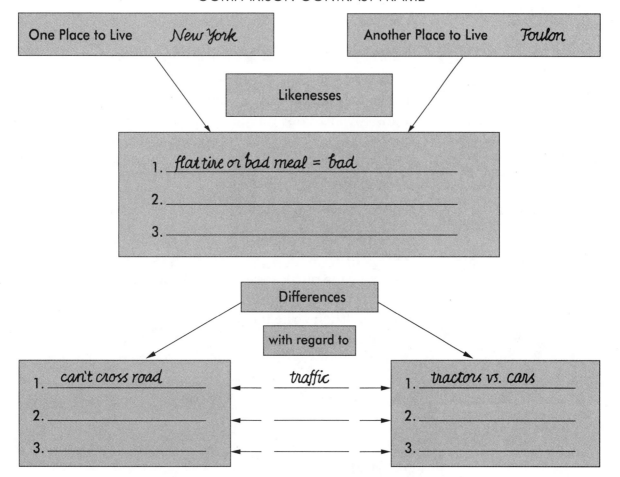

and the bad about each. Show the comparison and contrast clearly enough so that readers will know your choice at the end.

Thinking About the Model

When Andy Rooney compares two places to live, he does so kindly. He never really says anything bad about small towns. And the closest he comes to saying anything bad about a big city is by using the word "dirty" to describe it.

Still, the **comparison and contrast** is clear. You know the usual arguments, and you know Rooney's preference at the end.

Rooney lays out his ideas **part by part.** For instance, first he tells about the traffic in the small town and the big city. Then he goes on to other points.

CAPITALIZATION TIP

As you proofread, check capitalization. Since you are comparing two places to live, remember to capitalize the names of cities and states. Rooney writes about <u>T</u>oulon near the cities of <u>C</u>hicago, <u>P</u>eoria, and the town of <u>W</u>yoming.

PUNCTUATION TIP

When Rooney writes about cities and states, notice his use of commas. He follows the rule which says to use commas before and after the name of a state when it follows the names of a city. Rooney refers to Toulon, Illinois, (note the commas before and after *Illinois*) and the state of New Jersey (no commas without the city). Check your own writing.

Use your comparison-contrast frame to help you write the same kind of essay.

Writing Process Tip: Maintaining Consistent Tone

Once you decide on purpose and audience, you choose details to fit that purpose. Remember to keep the same attitude toward your topic throughout. For instance, Andy Rooney says, "I hit Toulon just right." Everything in that paragraph about Toulon is upbeat, cheerful, "just right." That is **consistent tone.**

As you write, try to keep the tone consistent.

Now Write

Review the purpose sentence you wrote in your learning log and the comparison-contrast frame you did on page 197. Then write the first draft of your paper. Make the comparisons and contrasts clear. Keep a consistent tone. And make sure readers know your position at the end.

When you finish the first draft, return to the lesson. You will use Rooney's writing as a model to help you revise.

REVISING

Checking Model's Map: Whole-by-Whole and Part-by-Part Plans

Comparison-contrast papers can be put together in two ways. One way is the way Andy Rooney did it: part by part.

In a part-by-part plan, you tell about traffic in the small town and traffic in the big city. Then you tell about homelessness in the small town and homelessness in the big city.

In a whole-by-whole plan, you tell everything about the small town. Then you tell everything about the big city. You give each a paragraph to itself.

Use the following exercises to apply what you know about comparison-contrast plans.

Then, check your paper. Can you improve the way you put your paper together?

TWO PLANS FOR COMPARISON-CONTRAST

Whole–by–whole plan

Paragraph 1

Topic A
Point 1
Point 2
Point 3

Paragraph 2

Topic B
Point 1
Point 2
Point 3

Part–by–part plan

Paragraph 1

Point 1
Topic A
Topic B

Paragraph 2

Point 2
Topic A
Topic B

Paragraph 3

Point 3
Topic A
Topic B

Exercise A—Comparing Apples and Apples

Directions. When you compare two places to live, you must compare similar ideas—apples and apples, not apples and oranges, so to speak. For example,

light traffic in small town and heavy traffic in big city (apples and apples)

light traffic in small town and airports in big city (apples and oranges)

In your learning log, number from 1 to 10. Study the following pairs of ideas. If it makes sense to compare them, write "okay" in your log. If it does not, revise one so that the comparison works.

On paper, design a Web site home page for the better place to live. Include buttons for several key features.

1. homeless shelters in big city and lack of homeless shelters in small town
2. unisex hair stylist in small town and bag ladies in large cities
3. tractor mechanic and auto mechanic
4. farming as a business and manufacturing as a business
5. arts-and-crafts shop and art gallery
6. theater district and county courthouse in the town square
7. ATM machine and twenty-six-story bank
8. cellular phone and television
9. McDonald's and Annie May's Diner
10. gravel road and city landfill

Exercise B—Choosing Comparisons

Directions. In your learning log, number from 1 to 10. Study the following groups of words that are based on Rooney's essay. In each group, two words or phrases show a clear comparison. Write those two in your log. The first one is done for you.

1. tractors, cows, fields, cars [tractors and cars]
2. flowers in yards, trash in gutter, cherry pie for dessert, flat tire
3. riding subway, walking to subway, riding tractor, waiting for bus
4. divided road, motel parking lot, two-car garage, two-lane street
5. street sweeper, homeless people, concerts, harrow
6. Broadway plays, swimming pools, multicultural population, European ancestry
7. Central Park, high-school basketball games, barn lot, NBA game
8. town square, homeless shelter, Civic Theater, theater district
9. shopping center, downtown district, town square, subway route
10. gourmet restaurant, Dairy Queen, Laundromat, ballpark

Exercise C—Creating Contrasts

Directions. In your learning log, number from 1 to 14. Below you will find fourteen numbered words. From the lettered list, find a contrasting word or words. Write the letter in your log. (There are more lettered words than you will use.)

1. loud	8. varied
2. dirty	9. interesting
3. crowded	10. strange
4. gritty	11. friendly
5. exciting	12. humorous
6. fulfilling	13. logical
7. sentimental	14. incredulous

a. sad	j. dull
b. impersonal	k. spotless
c. noisy	l. unemotional
d. quiet	m. ordinary
e. trusting	n. speedy
f. smooth	o. plain
g. musical	p. multicolored
h. unsatisfying	q. abandoned
I. logical	r. solid

Checking the Link: Links That Show Comparison and Contrast

Links help readers identify the comparisons or contrasts. Some words mean *different;* other words mean *the same.* For instance, these words signal readers that they will learn about differences:

but	not
by contrast	however
on the other hand	

These words signal readers that they will learn about similarities:

and	in the same way
also	likewise

Internet Connection

Many cities now have a home page on the Internet. It's often sponsored by the Chamber of Commerce or some other civic organization. Use a keyword search to locate possibly helpful information for your report.

Rooney also uses parallel parts to set up comparisons and contrasts. For instance,

> There are people who love Florida, people who hate Florida.

> There are those who love New York and those you couldn't pay enough to live in New York.

Like good connecting words, parallel parts set readers up for understanding comparisons and contrasts. Review Chapter 10 to help you remember how to set up parallel parts.

Use the following exercises to apply what you've learned about good links.

Exercise D—Links for Comparison-Contrast

Directions. In your learning log, number from 1 to 10. In the sentences below, identify the links that show comparisons or contrasts. Some sentences have more than one link. The first is done for you.

1. Toulon . . . is 125 miles southwest of Chicago, 40 miles northwest of Peoria and 7 miles from the town of Wyoming.

   Links: southwest, northwest, from

2. If you hit a place just right, you leave it with fond memories; but if you get a bad meal or a flat tire, you can turn against it forever.

3. There are people who love Florida, but there are also people who hate it.

4. There are those who love New York and those you couldn't pay enough to live in New York.

5. The biggest argument is whether it's best to live in the big city or the small town.

6. Everyone loves the small town, but in spite of all the talk, the movement is out of small towns and into the big cities.

7. Those who live in the city yearn for the country, but they don't move there.

8. When you fly over the wide open spaces of America or drive to a small town, it's hard to keep from wondering why people don't move.

Writing: An Art- and Literature-Based Approach

9. The homeless would still be homeless and the people already living in town wouldn't welcome them or have the facilities for helping them.

10. Can you live a fuller life and thus make life seem longer by going places, doing things and mingling with more interesting people in a big city?

Exercise E—Using Links for Comparison-Contrast

Directions. See the pictures on pages 190–191. In your learning log, number from 1 to 10. Leave three or four lines between the numbers.

Write two sentences for each item below. Use at least one link to show comparison-contrast.

1. Compare the row of houses in "Night Snow" with the rows of stalks in "Corn Field."

2. Contrast the view out the window in "New York City" with that in "Night Snow."

3. Contrast the building in "Home of the Brave" with that in "Ashanti Architecture."

4. Compare the seasons in "Corn Field" and "Night Snow."

5. Contrast the houses in "Ashanti Architecture" and "Night Snow."

6. Choose two pictures and compare or contrast what you think you would hear.

7. Choose two pictures and compare or contrast what you think you would smell.

8. Choose two pictures and compare or contrast the people who might live there.

9. Choose two pictures and compare or contrast the traffic you might find there.

10. Compare or contrast a photograph (such as "New York City" or "Corn Field") with a painting.

COMPUTER

If you have the equipment and software, plan a multimedia presentation. Create or scan in charts, graphs, photographs, illustrations, or maps, and add music. If you have a program like PowerPoint, you can project the computer material via an LCD panel or other projector. Be sure to practice your presentation before you address your audience.

HINT

Exercise F—Checking Consistent Tone

Directions. In your learning log, number from 1 to 10. Read the following sentences. Decide if each is consistent with Andy Rooney's tone. If so, write "consistent" in your log beside the sentence number. If not, write a revised sentence to make it consistent.

1. True, I didn't even get a flat tire in Toulon, but I hated the town anyway.
2. It was a lovely spring day and the dust from the harrowing choked me up.
3. Well-tended yards sprouted colorful flowers.
4. Every day the corner cafe served warm cinnamon buns with unlimited refills of coffee.
5. The waitress had the only scowl I saw all day.
6. The big city is crowded, dirty, gritty, and generally unpleasant.
7. The homeless people add to the misery of everyone in the big cities.
8. Big cities offer excitement, interesting people, and lots to do; but crime overrides the good.
9. A small town has its own forms of excitement and regular entertainment.
10. I love New York.

Exercise G—Checking Your Map

Directions. Before you wrote your first draft, you mapped out a comparison-contrast frame. Compare it with your draft. Did you follow your plan? Did you put comparisons together? Contrasts together? Make revisions as needed.

Peer-editor Activity. Ask a peer to read your paper and suggest at least one more comparison or contrast you can add. Make any needed revisions.

PROOFREADING

Right Reading: Avoiding Wordiness

A common problem with beginning writers is wordiness. Perhaps they've been told to "write one page" or to "write at least 100 words." So they add words to fill in.

Good writing uses strong nouns and verbs and few modifiers. (Remember what you learned in Chapter 1 about specific details.) Look at these examples:

The little toddler tumbled over and fell on her stomach. (wordy)

The toddler tumbled onto her stomach. (better)

The hot-water heater leaked water all over the basement floor. (wordy)

The water heater leaked over the basement floor. (better)

The following exercise lets you practice getting rid of wordiness.

Exercise H—Getting Rid of Wordiness

Directions. In your learning log, number from 1 to 10. Read the following sentences. Identify unneeded words. Then write the less wordy sentences in your log.

1. Andy Rooney is a person who loves New York.
2. It is probable that he nevertheless loved visiting Toulon.
3. The area surrounding Toulon is set aside for farming purposes.
4. Rooney talks about Toulon in a pleasant way.
5. Do you think he has decided the question as to whether he would live in Toulon or not?
6. The goal that he is working toward is to visit the small towns but live in the big cities.
7. In spite of the fact that he loves big cities, Rooney still enjoys the small town friendliness.
8. He would never admit that the crime conditions that exist in the big cities have become intolerable.
9. Rooney's fans know he is successful along the lines of being a clever writer and broadcaster.
10. There are two books by Rooney and I like them both.

Peer-editor Activity. Ask a peer to read your paper and check for wordiness. Make any needed revisions.

Census results are on the Net. You can find facts about cities at http://venus.census. gov/cdrom/lookup. Then click on "STF3C—Part 1: Nation and State Totals, Metropolitan Statistical Areas." Click on "Go to level Metropolitan Statistical Area" and then click on "Submit." Next, click on "Retrieve the areas you've selected below" and scroll to your city. Click on "Submit." Click on "Choose Tables to Retrieve" and then "Submit."

Worldwide information can be found in the CIA World Factbook at http://www.odci.gov/cia/ publications/95fact/index. html.
It is updated annually.

Final Draft

Prepare a final draft, making revisions and proofreading corrections. Use good form. Add a title that hints at, but does not name, the two places you compare.

Peer/Self-editing Chart

Use the following questions to check your final draft.

1. Did I show a clear comparison and contrast between two places to live?
2. Is my point of view clear at the end?
3. Did I use good linking words to show comparison and contrast?
4. Did I use parallel parts to emphasize comparisons and contrasts?
5. Did I get rid of excess words and repetition?
6. Did I keep a consistent tone?

Make any final corrections to your comparison paper before you share it with your audience.

SHARING

Prepare visuals to go with your work. Make drawings or find photos of the two places to live. Locate each on a map. You may want to use a chart or graph. When the visuals are ready, practice reading aloud. Then share your work with the class.

Portfolio Pointers

Put your final draft into your portfolio. Then, on a separate sheet of paper, answer the following questions:

1. What writing strength do I show in this assignment?
2. What was hardest for me and how did I overcome that?
3. What did I learn that I can use in another writing task?
4. If I did this assignment over, what would I do differently?
5. If I shared this paper with my adult relatives, what would I want them to notice about my writing?

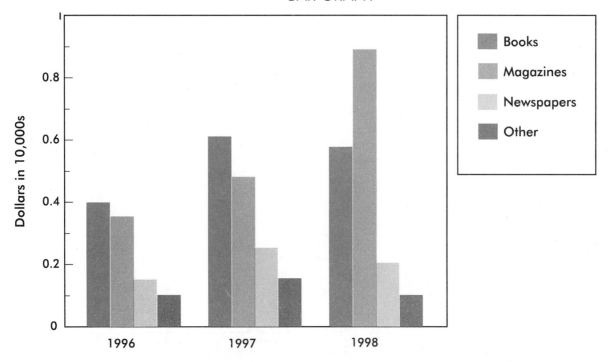

Relating Your Writing to the Workplace: Reading and Creating Graphs, Charts, and Tables

In the workplace, graphs, charts, and tables give the clearest comparisons or contrasts. A graph may compare this year's sales with those of last year. A chart may show how much money shoppers spend in each store of a shopping mall. A table may show how the weather affects spending.

The following graphs, charts, and tables all refer to business at a book store. All show comparisons. In a small group, discuss the graphs, charts, and tables and the comparisons they show. Use the following questions to guide you.

Study the bar graph above. What happened to the sale of books between 1996 and 1998? What other comparisons can you make from this graph?

Study the line graph. Which product showed the sharpest increase in sales between 1997 and 1998? What other comparisons can you make?

Notice that a pie chart can give the same information as

Comparing Two Places to Live

LINE GRAPH

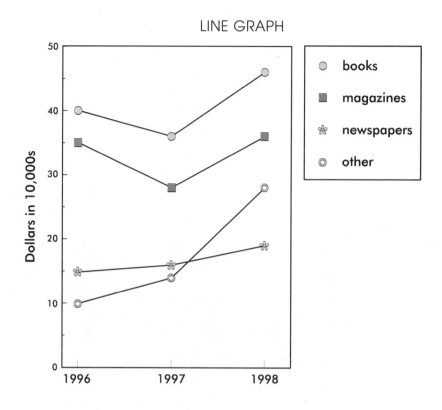

a line graph or bar graph. Look at the pie chart below. In what way is it better than either a bar graph or a line graph? In what way is it less good?

PIE CHART

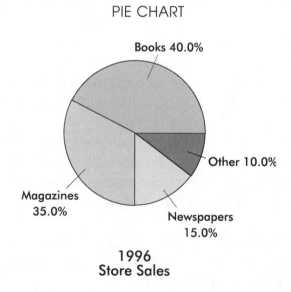

1996
Store Sales

A sales table like the one on the next page gives specific figures. Compare it with the pie chart. Which gives a clearer picture? Why?

Writing: An Art- and Literature-Based Approach

SALES TABLE

	books	magazines	newspapers	other
1996	40%	35%	15%	10%
1997	35%	40%	12%	13%
1998	46%	39%	10%	5%

Make your own comparison with real or imaginary details. Create a chart, graph, or table. Use the examples above as a model. Be ready to explain your comparison to the class.

Check the Atlas

Andy Rooney begins, "I just spent two days in Toulon." Study a map of Illinois. Locate Chicago. In what corner of the state is it? Toulon is, according to Rooney, 125 miles southwest of Chicago. Locate Toulon. Then find the other two towns he mentions (Peoria and Wyoming). Assuming Rooney flew out of Peoria to go home, how far is it from there to New York City? What states would he fly over? How close is New York City to New Jersey?

Interdisciplinary Interest Project: Profile of a City

Choose a city that interests you. You may want to choose a city where you once lived or one where you think you might like to live. You may want to choose the one you live in now.

Create a profile of the city. Include such vital statistics as population, employment, business opportunities, schools and universities, transportation, communication, per capita income, health facilities, recreation, cost of living, and so forth.

To find that information, consult the most recent census statistics for that city. The census is taken every ten years, and your public library should have the information. Use a KWL chart like the one below to guide you.

Comparing Two Places to Live

Present your findings to the class. Avoid a dry list of the numbers. Instead, talk about why the city would or would not be a good place to live.

KWL CHART

Subject		
K What I Know	**W** What I Want to Know	**L** What I Learned

Writing: An Art- and Literature-Based Approach

chapter 12

Writing

for Laughs

PREWRITING

Visuals

1. "Laid Back" by Gloria Graham
2. "Time Transfixed" by René Magritte
3. "Carnival in Arcueil" by Lyonel Feininger
4. "Herringboned" by William Wegman
5. "Mis Hijos" by Elizabeth Catlett

"Among those whom I like, I can find no common denominator, but among those whom I love, I can; all of them make me laugh."

W. H. Auden, author
The Dyer's Hand

Your Viewer's Response

Choose one of the pictures. Or choose one from another source. What does it remind you of that makes you laugh? In your learning log, write two sentences. In the first sentence, tell who, what, when, and where. In the second sentence, tell why that memory made you laugh.

> EXAMPLE:
> Last Friday night, my dad met my older sister's date at the front door. Dad told the guy Sis was on the phone lining up a date for Saturday night.

Herringboned by William Wegman

Carnival in Arcueil
by Lyonel Feininger

Time Transfixed by René Magritte

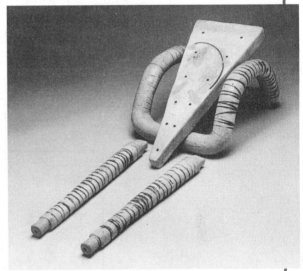

Laid Back by Gloria Graham

Mis Hijos by Elizabeth Catlett

The following selection is great for laughs. The humor results from **juxtaposition**—putting one idea next to another—to show the comedy.

About the Author

Top-paid comedian Bill Cosby (1937–) was the first African-American actor to star in a dramatic series on television. While he has earned several Emmy awards, he has also put his comedy in written form.

Vocabulary

yacht (YAHT) n. a boat for pleasure cruises

Excerpt From

THEY'RE TALKING ABOUT A FIELD TRIP TO FRANCE

by Bill Cosby

from *Childhood*

Children today seem to need considerably more guidance than I received. In fact, the heart of the modern school is not the cafeteria or the parking lot: it's the detention room, a minimum-security lounge designed to teach ethics to kids while keeping their social contacts fresh.

"Detention was really fun today," my son Ennis once told me, as if talking about a yacht club. "All the best people were there."

"I thought it was supposed to be for *punishment*," I said.

"Oh, it can be for that too—if your friends aren't there or if Mrs. Piano is in a bad mood."

"She's the warden?"

"That's funny, Dad. They'd love you in detention because they love to have a good laugh."

"Yes, every prison needs some laughs. Tell me, why did you happen to get this particular honor today?"

"Dad, detention isn't anything bad."

"Sorry; I've been confused. So why were you invited to cocktails there?"

"Dad, you kill me."

"Don't rule it out."

"Well, *today's* detention—"

"You get it every day?"

"I told you: it's nothing bad. Maybe it was in the Middle Ages, but believe me, it's changed."

"I believe you."

"Today I got it just for throwing a book at James in history. Can you imagine that? Mr. Weinstock gave it to me just for throwing a book. I mean, a *grenade* I could understand."

"Just for throwing your history book."

"Oh no, I don't have one of those."

"You're waiting for it to come as the Book-of-the-Month?"

"No, I lent it to Aaron."

"*And?*"

"Well, he's trying hard to remember what he did with it. We've definitely ruled out his locker 'cause there's no more room in there; and he doesn't think he left it at the mall."

"That's where I'd look for it."

Your Reader's Response

With a partner, imagine that you are Cosby and his son, Ennis. Continue the conversation.

DIALOGUE FLOWCHART

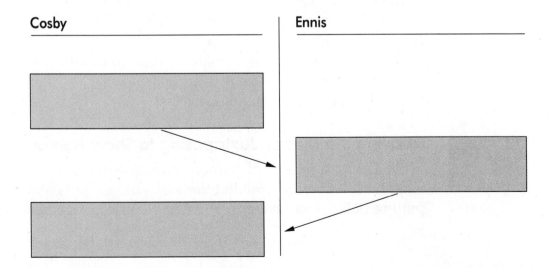

Cosby

Ennis

Springboards for Writing

Use one or both of the following activities to help you think of writing ideas.

Individual Activity. Skim the cartoon page from a newspaper. Identify five funny cartoon strips. Decide who says the punch lines. Do all characters say something funny? Or is one character the "straight guy" and the other gets the laughs? What makes the lines funny? Share what you find with the class. Be sure everyone can see each strip as you talk about it.

Group Activity. Bill Cosby and his son make a typical comedy team. Ennis is the "straight guy" and Cosby delivers the punch lines. In groups or as a class, name other comedy teams. If possible, view videos of some of the famous teams. Follow the dialogue. What makes the routine funny?

In groups or as a class, name other generic comedy teams, such as the coach and his assistant or the principal and your father.

Now Decide

From your Viewer's Response, Reader's Response, or the activities above, pick two characters—real or imaginary—who can be funny together. Think about a situation in which you can put them.

Then write three sentences in your learning log. The first should name the characters and tell how they are connected (such as a coach and his assistant or the principal and your father).

The second should name the place and time (such as in the locker room during half-time, or in the principal's office after school).

The third should name the situation (such as after the assistant coach orders pizza during half-time, or after you've been in trouble in English class).

Studying the Model: Juxtaposing to Show Humor

Bill Cosby, a master of humor, puts ideas together in ways that most of us wouldn't think of. His humor is like putting polka dots, stripes, plaids, and paisleys together in one outfit. He refers, for instance, to the detention room as a minimum-security lounge.

The words "minimum-security" and "lounge" don't fit together, since "minimum-security" usually refers to prisons and "lounge" usually refers to a place for relaxation.

Cosby also puts "detention" with "yacht club," and his son Ennis says, "All the best people were there."

Again, the ideas don't fit together. So they're funny.

Putting ideas together that way is called **juxtaposition.** There's nothing funny about a detention room, there's nothing funny about minimum security, and there's nothing funny about a lounge. But juxtaposed, they're funny!

Juxtaposing can also create exaggeration, like referring to Cosby's schooling during "the Middle Ages."

In your learning log or with a peer, make a list of the juxtapositions you find in Cosby's writing. About how often does juxtaposition occur in this passage? What does that tell you about writing your own humor?

Mapping Your Writing: Brainstorm with a Detail Chart

To help you brainstorm ideas for your humorous story, use the detail chart below. Name the two characters in the center. Name details that could be funny as they interact.

PUNCTUATION TIP

Grammatically speaking, the juxtaposed words Cosby uses are *nonessential*. In other words, they are not essential to the factual meaning but add humor or give additional information.

Set off nonessential word groups with commas. For example:

> Ennis was assigned to the detention room, *which Cosby calls a minimum-security lounge.*

> The detention room, *which Ennis sees as a place for fun,* is supposed to be for punishment.

The italicized word groups are added information. They are not essential for the meaning of the sentence. Thus, they are set off with commas.

DETAIL CHART

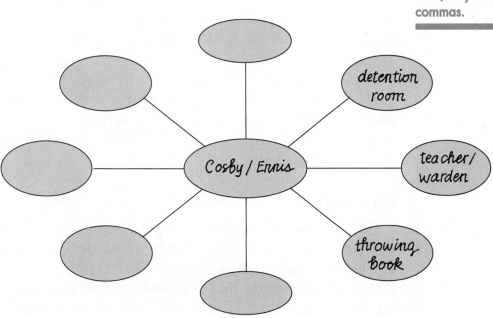

WRITING

Your Assignment

Write a humorous piece. Choose an everyday topic, like Bill Cosby's talk with his son about school. Use juxtaposition to create laughs.

Thinking About the Model

The **juxtaposition** Bill Cosby uses makes his writing as humorous as his television shows.

Sometimes the juxtaposition is a play on words. For instance, when Ennis says of his father, "You kill me," he is referring of course to the expression used when something is really funny.

However, when Cosby replies, "Don't rule it out," he is responding to another meaning of "kill."

Note, too, that Cosby's juxtapositions are usually in dialogue. Review Chapter 8, "Writing a Conversation," to help you remember how to write good dialogue.

Try to model your own humor after Cosby's. Make sure every **part fits the total** picture—humor!

Writing Process Tip: Sharing

The final step of the writing process is that of **sharing.** When your writing is finished and polished, it's time to present it to your audience. Bill Cosby's audience is huge, and many of you have probably been part of it. On the other hand, your own audience may be small, but it's just as important.

Think about ways to expand your audience. Is your topic suitable for a letter to the editor of your school newspaper or literary magazine? Can you submit it to a contest? Send it to a friend? Put it on the bulletin board? Share it with another class?

Now Write

With an audience in mind, use your learning log notes and your detail chart to write the first draft of your paper. Use juxtaposition to create humor.

When you finish the first draft, return to the lesson. You will use Cosby's writing as a model to help you revise.

COMPUTER

One of the easiest ways to share your work is to send it electronically through a network or through e-mail to other classes, perhaps in other buildings.

To reach a larger audience, put your work on the Internet. Ask for responses.

One group of students in Ohio wrote haiku (short poems) for fellow students in Japan. The Japanese students wrote back. Through translators, each group learned not only more about the Japanese form of poetry but also about each other.

Sharing your work electronically may have similar rewards.

HINT

REVISING

Checking Model's Map: Making the Pieces Fit the Total Picture

Cosby's writing is like a jigsaw puzzle. All of the pieces fit into the picture, and when the picture is done, there are no pieces left over. Every detail adds to the humor about detention.

All good writing—humorous or not—should fit together the same way. For instance, if your purpose is to be humorous, then nothing should take away from the humor. If your purpose is to sell an idea, then nothing should take away from the sale. If your purpose is to describe an event, then nothing should take away from the description.

In your learning log, use the detail chart on page 217 to chart the pieces of Cosby's jigsaw puzzle.

Use the following exercises to apply what you've learned. Then, revise your writing as needed. Make sure the details give the whole picture. And make sure you have no details left over.

Exercise A—Identifying Details That Don't Fit the Picture

Directions. In your learning log, number from 1 to 10. Study the groups of words below. They represent something that Ennis would study, use, or experience as a student. In each group, one detail does not fit the picture. Write that detail in your log and tell why it does not fit. Some may have more than one correct answer. The first is done for you.

1. history, math, science, lunch, English [Lunch is not a school subject.]
2. shirt, jacket, gloves, coat, sweater
3. paper, computer, printer, floppy disk, mouse
4. soccer, baseball, tennis, football, track, basketball
5. eating, farming, laughing, breathing, talking, thinking
6. automobile, bed, chair, dresser, sofa, table
7. blizzard, cyclone, gale, hurricane, shelter, typhoon

Cosby uses numerous words with *ie* or *ei* letters, such as *field* trip, *received* guidance, *their* contacts, absent *friends*, and *believe* me.

An easy rule helps you remember whether it's *ie* or *ei:* Put *i* before *e* except after *c* or when it sounds like *a* as in *neighbor* and *weigh*.

As you proofread, check your own work for *ie* and *ei* words.

8. blush, frown, hate, smile, stare
9. comma, explanation point, paragraph, period, quotation marks, semicolon
10. anger, fear, joy, sadness, worry, memory

Exercise B—Adding a Detail to Fit the Picture

Directions. In your learning log, number from 1 to 10. Read the word groups below. They represent subjects Ennis may be studying or activities in which he may be involved. In each group, add one more detail that will fit the picture, and identify the picture. Write it in your log. The first is done for you.

1. cheering, clapping, stomping [screaming, as fans at a sporting event]
2. laughing, chuckling, smiling
3. Middle Ages, Renaissance, Victorian Era
4. World War II, Korean War, Vietnam War
5. sparrows, finches, warblers
6. fractions, whole numbers, decimals
7. note taking, note writing, note passing
8. library, cafeteria, classroom
9. books, book bag, notebooks
10. calculator, computer, printer

Peer-editor Activity. Ask a peer to read your draft with you to check the parts of the puzzle. Do all of the pieces fit? Do you have pieces left over? Revise as needed.

Checking the Links: Using Links for Humor

Humor is the most sophisticated kind of writing you will be asked to do. As a result, everything you have studied in this book will help you. And every linking word or word group you have studied will help you write good humor.

Cosby uses many of them. For example, he uses four linking words in the second sentence:

> *In fact,* the heart of the modern school is *not* the cafeteria *or* the parking lot: it's the detention room, a min-

imum-security lounge designed to teach ethics to kids *while* keeping their social contacts fresh.

Use the following exercises to find good links.

Exercise C—Studying Cosby's Links

Directions. In your learning log, number from 1 to 10. Find the linking words and word groups in these sentences. Write them in your log.

1. "Detention was really fun today," my son Ennis once told me.
2. "I thought it was supposed to be for punishment," I said. "Oh, it can be for that too," Ennis replied.
3. "It's punishment if your friends aren't there or if Mrs. Piano is in a bad mood."
4. "They'd love you in detention because they love to have a good laugh."
5. "Sorry; I've been confused. So why were you invited to cocktails there?"
6. "Maybe detention was bad in the Middle Ages, but believe me, it's changed."
7. "Today I got detention just for throwing a book at James."
8. "Oh, no, I don't have a history book."
9. "We've definitely ruled out his locker because there's no more room in there."
10. "We've ruled out his locker, and he doesn't think he left it at the mall."

Exercise D—Adding Links

Directions. In your learning log, number from 1 to 10. In the following sentences, add a linking word or word group to connect ideas. Use a different link in each sentence.

1. Cosby thinks today's schools differ from those in his day; _____ he never thought of detention as fun.
2. Detention _____ yacht clubs didn't have the same atmosphere.
3. _____, it was punishment to be sent to detention.

4. Depending on the teacher, _____, some detention days were better than others.

5. Throwing a book is bad, _____ throwing a grenade would be much worse.

6. Ennis threw a book; _____, he was sent to detention again.

7. _____, his father learned that Ennis' history book was missing.

8. Ennis and Aaron can't find the book; _____, they don't worry about its loss.

9. Cosby, _____, is worried about the loss.

10. He's worried _____ he may have to buy another one.

Peer-editor Activity. Ask a peer to read your draft with you. Together, highlight the linking words and word groups. Do you have links in almost every sentence? Revise as needed.

Exercise E—Studying Juxtaposition

Directions. See the pictures on pages 212–213. In your learning log, number from 1 to 5. Name the humorous juxtaposition in each picture.

Exercise F—Juxtaposition for Humor

Directions. Before you wrote your first draft, you made a detail map listing ideas you might use. Compare it with your draft. Did you use all or most of the details? Can you add others?

Now think about juxtaposing the details with others to add humor. Can you think of others?

Revise as needed.

Peer-editor Activity. Ask a peer to read your draft with you. Perhaps he or she can help you think of details to juxtapose to add humor. Revise as needed.

PROOFREADING

Right Reading: Misplaced Modifiers

I saw Cosby leave before the sun came up in a red car.

If you read that sentence carefully, it surely made you smile. Since when does the sun come up in a red car?

The problem is a misplaced modifier. The group of words *in a red car* is placed next to *sun* and seems to refer to *sun*. Instead, of course, it refers to *leave.* The modifier is misplaced. It should read,

> I saw Cosby leave in a red car before the sun came up.

Or,

> Before the sun came up, I saw Cosby leave in a red car.

Such sentences create humor—but not the kind of humor you want!

Use the following exercises to practice finding and fixing misplaced modifiers.

Exercise G—Recognizing Misplaced Modifiers

Directions. In your learning log, number from 1 to 10. Some of the following sentences have misplaced modifiers. If they do, write "misplaced" in your log. If they do not, write "okay."

1. The Emmy Award was given to Cosby who has had a great television comedy series as a symbol of his fans' love.
2. Ennis, be sure you have enough paper to finish your assignment before you start working.
3. Did you know they are trying to make injury-proof helmets for football players made of plastic?
4. I snuggled in to watch videos of my favorite Cosby shows wearing sweatpants and a T-shirt.
5. The Cosby fan club will send a picture of Cosby at work on his next book for a small fee.
6. Ennis was given two weeks' detention for a long list of faults by his history teacher.
7. Cosby sent a note to the teacher who had tried to instill a sense of ethics in Ennis by mail.
8. Assigned to detention, the teacher was frustrated by the ill-mannered students.

Sometimes humor hinges on the intentional misuse of a word:

> She doesn't have voice mail, only voice female.

The humor comes from the intentional use of the homonym *mail* for *male* and the pairing of it with *female.* Unintentional spelling errors, however, detract from the humor. Be sure you proofread carefully.

Remember, your spell checker cannot find incorrect words, only incorrect spellings.

9. Having lost his book, history class no longer made sense to Ennis.

10. Losing his sense of humor, Cosby told Ennis he'd better find his book.

Exercise H—Correcting Misplaced Modifiers

Directions. Review the sentences in Exercise G. For each sentence with a misplaced modifier, write a revision to correct it. Put the revisions in your learning log.

Peer-editor Activity. Ask a peer to review your humorous writing. Can he or she spot any misplaced modifiers? Revise as needed.

Final Draft

Prepare a final draft, making revisions and proofreading corrections. Use good form. Add a title that, like Cosby's, hints at the humor.

Peer/Self-editing Chart

Use the following questions to check your final draft.

1. Did I use juxtaposition to create humor?
2. Did I use what I know about parallel parts to add to the humor?
3. Did I use what I know about all kinds of linking words and word groups to connect ideas?
4. Did I use what I know about writing good conversation to add to the humor?
5. Did I avoid misplaced modifiers?
6. Have I applied the other writing skills that I learned?

Make final corrections to your humorous paper before you share it with your audience.

SHARING

Humor begs for an audience. Use video or audio tape to record yours. Add sound effects, including "canned" or real laughter. Send the completed tapes to a retirement home, nursing home, or senior citizens' center.

COMPUTER

Technology can make a good presentation even better. Explore the choices you have on your hardware and software. Can you project on a large screen what you have on your computer monitor? If so, you can use computer graphics during your presentation. Check to see what other capabilities your equipment may have.

HINT

Writing: An Art- and Literature-Based Approach

Portfolio Pointers

Put your final draft into your portfolio. Then, on a separate sheet of paper, answer the following questions:

1. What strengths does this paper show?
2. What did I use from other chapters to help me do this assignment?
3. What did I learn about writing from others?

Relating Your Writing to the Workplace: Making a Presentation

The final step of the writing process is sharing or publishing. In the workplace, you must be able to present information to colleagues, customers, and clients. What you say needs to inform or convince.

Talk to an adult in the workplace who can tell you about the kinds of presentations he or she must make. Learn as much as you can about the who, what, where, when, and why of the presentations.

Give a class presentation explaining what you learned. Remember to use good speaking skills and visuals where appropriate (such as charts, graphs, and tables).

Check the Atlas

The title of Cosby's work illustrates his brand of humor: "They're Talking about a Field Trip to France." On a map, locate France. What countries border France? If you were flying from your home to France, what states and countries would you cross?

Interdisciplinary Interest Project: Field Trip to France

The chapter from which Bill Cosby's comedy piece was taken is titled "They're Talking about a Field Trip to France." Imagine that your class wants to take a field trip to France—or to some other equally distant place. Write a proposal for your school board seeking their approval for the trip. Include in your proposal the purpose of the trip, an itinerary, transportation arrangements, housing and meal plans, cost per student, and detailed plans for raising money to meet the cost.

Skills Chart

Chapter	Model: Author, Title	Lesson from the Model	Prewriting: Mapping Your Writing	Writing Process Tip	Revising: Checking Model's Map	Links (Transitions)	Proofreading
1. Finding Something to Write About	Charles Kuralt: from *A Life on the Road*	Specific details	Cluster map	Choosing a topic; forming a topic sentence	Specific details to explain general ideas	Linking words and phrases	Complete sentences
2. Keeping a Reflective Journal	Rose Fosdick: "Chicken Hill" and "Cape Nome"	Time order	Sequence chart; sunburst chart	Focusing on Audience	Plotting time order	Words to show time order	Subject-verb agreement
3. Telling What You Hear, See, Smell, Taste, and Feel	Yoshiko Uchida: "Tub under the Stars"	Sensory language	Sensory language chart	Deciding on purpose	Unity	Repetition	Noun-pronoun agreement; clear pronoun reference
4. Describing a Place You Like	N. Scott Momaday from *The Way to Rainy Mountain*	Similes and metaphors	Sameness organizer; space order map	Narrowing your topic	Plotting space order	Words to show space order	Possessive forms
5. Telling about Someone You Know	Eugenia W. Collier: "Marigolds"	Sentence variety: beginnings	Character Chart	Gathering details	Logical order	Sentence beginnings for logical order	Punctuating introductory elements
6. Telling a True Story	B. and M. Ashabranner: from "Most Vulnerable People"	Sentence variety: length	Story map	Choosing details	Step by step	Phrases that show step by step	Punctuating to avoid run-ons
7. Sharing a Learning Experience	Rudolpho Anaya: from *Bless Me, Ultima*	Compound parts	Sequence chart	Developing topic sentences	Compounds showing similarities, differences	Showing likeness and difference	Punctuating compound parts and series
8. Writing a Conversation	Maya Angelou: from *I Know Why Caged Bird Sings*	Paragraphing in dialog	Dialog flow chart	Forming implied topic sentences	Whole and part in dialog	Tag lines in dialog	Punctuating dialog
9. Giving Personality to the Wind	Ann Petry: from *The Street*	Strong verbs	Cause and effect frame	Writing concluding sentences	Cause and effect	Showing cause and effect relationships	Verbs tenses and shifts
10. Writing a Travel Piece	B. Ashabranner: from "I Get Aggravated, Nervous in Town"	Parallelism	Classification chart	Making the logic clear	Classifying details	Connecting parallel parts	Using like grammatical parts
11. Comparing Two Places to Live	Andrew Rooney: "Big City Blues"	Showing comparison and contrast	Comparison-contrast frame	Maintaining Consistent Tone	Whole-by-whole and part-by-part	Words and phrases to show comparison-contrast	Wordiness and redundancy
12. Writing for Laughs	Bill Cosby: from "They're Talking about a Field Trip to France"	Juxtaposition to create humor	Detail chart	Publishing and Presenting	Making parts fit the total	Links to aid humor	Misplaced and dangling modifiers

Writing: An Art- and Literature-Based Approach

Punctuation Tip	Spelling Tip	Capitalization Tip	Inter-disciplinary Link	Workplace Skill	Computer Hints	Internet Connection
Parenthetical links	One or two words or hyphenated, -ed/-ing endings on verbs	Common / proper nouns	Return from Vietnam War	Learning on your own	Word processing, spell check, e-mail, revising, thesaurus, style checkers, check fragments, CD-ROM references	career sites
Introductory clauses, phrases	Contractions	Titles of people	Native foods in your backyard	Mapping a work day	Line-draw software, files and disks, portfolio disk	chat room, map sites
Appositives; quotation marks and underscore/ italics of titles	Homonyms: *their/there/ they're* and *its/it's*	Titles of artistic works	World War II U.S.-Japanese camps	Using technical language	Thesaurus for vocabulary study, word counts, style checker, avoiding repetition, technical language in manuals	Internet print directories
Apostrophes with possessives and contractions	Plurals and possessives with apostrophes	Geographic terms and names of celestial bodies	Learning about the Kiowas	Making the complex simple	Line-draw software, print copy, logical file directory, block command, CD-ROM reference	Destination sites, Native American Art and Education Center site
Introductory elements: word, phrase, clause	Adding suffixes to words ending in silent *e*	Common and proper adjectives	Raising annuals	Creating a logical filing system	CD-ROM references, character bins, graphics, block command, undo, alphabetical and sequential orders, computer garden plan	
Commas with introductory links	-cede, -ceed, -sede	First word of a sentence; people and languages	Boat people and other refugees	Giving Directions for a Process	Word counts, sentence-length/count, graph, multiple columns, keyword searches in CD-ROMs	Web browser, Vietnamese Boat People site
Commas w/coordinate adjectives, compound sentences, series	Letter *c* pronounced *s* or *k*	School subjects	Plants and herbal remedies	Keeping a Daily Work Log	Thesaurus for antonyms, CD-ROM quotations, page breaks w/topic sentences	Reference works, quotations
Punctuating dialog	Roots; purposeful misspelling in dialog	Capitalization in dialog	Poetry of Presidential Inaugurations	Dialog with the Boss	Networked group, caps lock in dialog thesaurus for tags, scan text to format, order of punctuation marks	Art sites, White House address
Commas vs. semicolons	Homonyms; irregular verbs	Personification	Cause of wind and its effects	Showing a telephone personality	On-line vs. CD-ROM thesaurus, copy/paste, word bins, transition checker	
Commas with parallel series	Prefixes	Points of the compass vs. geographic regions	Animals native to the Southwest	Using Map Skills at Work	Transition checkers, highlighting links, presentation with computer projection	U.S. Customs Web site, sites for travel destinations, travel means
Commas with linking words, cities and states	Spell-checker warning	Cities and states	Profile of a city	Reading and making graphs, charts, and tables	Block command to reorganize, cut/paste, multimedia presentations	Art sites, home pages, CNN, city sites, U.S. Census, USA/World Factbook sites
Commas with nonessential items	-ie vs. -ei; spelling for humor	Businesses and organizations	Field trip to France	Making a presentation	Idea wheels, sharing via e-mail, multimedia presentations	Humor on the Net, Dr. Seuss site, World Factbook re: France

Skills Chart

Index